Pearl Buck's America

Pearl Buck's America

Text by Pearl S. Buck
Photographs from *Life*

BARTHOLOMEW
HOUSE
LTD

BARTHOLOMEW HOUSE LTD.

First Printing November 1971
© 1971 by Pearl S. Buck and Lyle Kenyon Engel
Library of Congress Catalog Card Number: 70-173298
International Standard Book Number: 0-87794-029-0

Pearl Buck's America
     Produced by Lyle Kenyon Engel
          Editors: Marla Ray
                    George Engel
Book designed by Fred Hausman

This book is dedicated to my people,
the people of the United States of America,
with the hope and the belief
that they will lead the way
to world peace and friendship.

CONTENTS

THE PHOTOGRAPHERS

Lee Balterman
Margaret Bourke-White
Gerald Brimacombe
Edward Clark
Joseph Clark
Ralph Crane
Myron Davis
Loomis Dean
John Dominis
Alfred Eisenstaedt
Eliot Elisofon
J. R. Eyerman
N. R. Farbman
Albert Fenn
Andreas Feininger
Herbert Gehr
Bob Gomel
Fritz Goro
Allan Grant
Henry Groskinsky
Henry Grossman
Otto Hagel
Carl Iwasaki
Yale Joel
Robert W. Kelley
Dmitri Kessel
Wallace Kirkland

Nina Leen
John Leongard
Leonard McCombe
Francis Miller
Ralph Morse
A. Y. Owen
Lynn Pelham
Charles Phillips
Bill Ray
Co Rentmeester
Arthur Rickerby
Michael Rougier
Walter Sanders
Arthur Schatz
Frank Scherschel
Joseph Scherschel
Paul Schutzer
George Silk
George Skadding
Howard Sochurek
W. Eugene Smith
Peter Stackpole
Gordon Tenney
Grey Villet
Hank Walker
James Whitmore
John Zimmerman

This book is a personal communication between my country and me. I did not know my country until half my life had gone by. Then with adult mind and willing heart, I came here to live. All was new, all was wonderful, nearly all was beautiful. I wonder if Americans who have always lived here know how beautiful our country is? We take our own beauty for granted, I think! Yet traveling as I have over its great expanse, visiting one state and another, always with a purpose of my own, I have seen such wondrous sights that, were they in some ancient Asian land, they would be places of worship since, the Asians would say, such beauty must be the site of gods. Yet we Americans come and go, for work or pleasure, accepting the beauty almost without wonder, as our natural environment.

I am not saying that our people are insensitive and without the gift of wonder. Beauty, however, we have as our endowment, and it does not surprise me, as once it did, when abroad I used to be sometimes mortified that a fellow American failed to be properly impressed with, in my opinion, some famous Asian sight. We Americans have more than our share of the world's wonders.

It would be impossible for me, therefore, to write of all there is to see. I can only write of what I myself have seen and felt about my country. I do not even write chronologically or in geographic order. Let guidebooks furnish travel information. I write of what it means to me, now, in the accumulation of the years. But I write of more than landscapes. I write, too, of the people. My memory is crowded with people I have met, high and low, simple and complex, young and old. For it is noble people and good, as well as beautiful land, who make a country noble and beautiful.

America is vast. America stretches from east to west, from the Atlantic Ocean to the Pacific. But I am accustomed to immense countries. I was reared from birth to adulthood in a country even more vast than the United States. I am accustomed to immensity in lands and peoples.

America is beautiful. But I have been steeped in beauty all my life long. Asia is richly beautiful, diversely beautiful, and its beauty is centuries old. Yet I cling to my own country. Why? I wonder why. Is it because my parents, living on the other side of the world, so far away from home, infused me with their memories and dreams? Something of this is true, doubtless. But I have lived in my country long enough now so that I have my own memories and dreams. I do not depend upon others. I need not depend even upon books. I can write my own books about my own country and my own people now. I have experienced enough, seen enough, felt enough to know for myself.

Though I came as a stranger to my country, having lived in China since my birth, nevertheless I was actually born in the United States. I like the combination. To be born in a country provides a natural anchor there, and I am permanently American.

To return as a stranger, however, also has its advantages. I see my own country with the sharply observing eyes of a stranger. Everything is new to me. There are no memories to blur the edges. I see my country whole.

ALABAMA

Alabama, for some reason I cannot determine, seems to me to be the most southern State of the South. An air of the past hovers about it still. Perhaps it is because the houses I have visited there are old plantation homes, where quiet, civilized people live very much as their forefathers lived, except that slavery is no more. Yet the people who serve in those great houses are the descendants of slaves, they are free and are paid good wages, they serve with the grace of good manners and deference, and their employers treat them well and with deserved appreciation.

There is an air of old culture in these houses. Though some of the young people dress flamboyantly and defy their elders by wearing long hair and short skirts, there is still about them the air of distinction born of ancestors who knew their Latin and Greek as a matter of course, and who took the grand tour to Europe as a finishing touch to their education. The lovely gardens of Montgomery and Mobile provide a dream-like refuge from today's racial strife and aggressive young businessmen. The quietly wealthy aristocrats of Alabama live in an atmosphere of good music, good libraries and good food.

And yet there is a quite different Alabama. Political and racial strife have torn the state apart ever since Montgomery, where the Confederate states organized, became the first capital of the Confederacy. The racial issue continues in the difficult transition from past to present. There is a curious love-hate relationship between the black and the white, born of past mutual dependence upon one another. They understand each other, they need each other, and yet they have not found a satisfactory way to express their mutual needs and make them serve the present.

In the old days, of course, the relationship was clear. The economy of Alabama depended then on cotton and cotton depended on slave workers. Modern machinery and electric power industrialized even the cotton fields, however, and the black people were forced to compete with the poor white in the new age. The relationship changed abruptly. Today life in Alabama no longer centers in baronial plantations and great old houses. A new and vigorous life has come to the dignified old state. This new life centers around the blast furnaces of Birmingham and the cotton empire around Montgomery. The waters of the Tennessee River, gathered and directed in power, have made the transition from past to present, and today's vigorous young businessmen are the new age's directors. The spearhead of this new age is to be found in the Space Flight Center in Huntsville and its thrust into the universe.

All this has taken place in a state of mild, almost tropical climate, a gentle state whose northern scenery is rolling hills and gem-like lakes, and whose south faces the warm Mexican Gulf waters. It lives a vigorous modern life, and yet there is an undying sense of history. It was the fourth state to secede from the Union, and Jefferson Davis was inaugurated in Montgomery on February 18, 1861. Alabama men fought on every Confederate front, although twenty-five white and ten thousand black men fought on the side of the Union. A most bitter memory of the past still lingers from the cruelty of the carpetbaggers who moved in on the defeated South, perhaps most cruelly in Alabama. But by 1880, the worst was over. It was then that Birmingham began in earnest to develop its steel industry from the iron ore in its northern areas. And Mobile became a great port.

Yes, it is a busy port but what I recall are the famous azalea gardens and the glory and amusements of its Mardi Gras. A few specifics—Athens, too, is a lovely town, and I remember its handsome Greek Revival houses dignifying its ancient Greek name. It was the first community to suffer

in the Civil War and, curious contrast, the first Alabama city to get TVA electricity. And the town of Bessemer was so named after the great English steelmaker, although De Bardeleken, who first made steel here, did not use the Bessemer method. And Dauphin Island, thirty miles south of Mobile in the Gulf of Mexico, is a heavenly place for recreation now, although on August 5, 1864, Admiral David Farragut used it as a base for his cannon and so began the Battle of Mobile Bay. But long before that, Spaniards had settled there and from here Mobile was born. And peanuts are celebrated in Enterprise by a monument in the public square dedicated to the boll weevil, because this pest made peanuts more profitable than cotton. And at Horseshoe Bend there is a National Military Park. Hernando de Soto, the Spaniard, had explored here in early expeditions and discovered a communal-rural society of Creek Indians. When Horseshoe Bend was founded in 1814 by General Andrew Jackson's final victory, the Creeks moved to Oklahoma. And at Russell Cave National Monument are findings of Stone Age human beings who had made a strange underground home in a huge cavern and left their debris there. Scientists date the life in this cave at 7,000 B.C. And finally let me mention Tuskeegee, where once I visited George Washington Carver when he was already very old, but not too old to explain to me very clearly his great scientific contributions.

A lovely state, this Alabama, in spite of wars and dissensions in past and present; somehow one has the conviction that, past and present, its problems will be solved.

ALASKA

My personal contacts with this huge State have been twofold: first, a friendship with a former governor, Ernest Gruening, who was a warm friend of my husband's; and second, a young Amerasian, father Chinese, mother Polish-American, who grew up under my sponsorship, entered a career in the Coast Guard, married a Pennsylvania Dutch girl and in the course of duty lived for some years in Alaska, long enough to experience the recent earthquake there. Thus through the eyes of a governor and a coastguardsman, I have seen Alaska although I have never been there.

What have I learned? Many facts and feelings! First among the facts was the incredible bargain the United States made when she purchased Alaska from Russia for a mere $7,200,000. True, there were many people who, understanding nothing of the future potential of this magnificent area, called the purchase folly. Nothing could have been more mistaken. Imagine, if you can, what it might have meant if Russia had retained this strong foothold on our continent! As it is, we have instead a point of potential for the

future which we may use if we like. Alaska is our nearest land area to Asia. Conceivably there might be a bridge built there some day to facilitate travel between the continents. Today it remains a window toward Asia rather than serving as a gate, and the bridge may never be built. Yet again it may—who knows in this era when the incredible so often becomes the possible?

Meanwhile, Alaska is developing its own potential. The state is fast promoting its modern growth with airlines, highways, telegraph and telephone systems. But Americans know too little of our forty-ninth state. We think of her as one at a distance, or perhaps only as a newcomer whose potential is not yet clear. This is a mistake, however. Many Americans moved into Alaska, partly to escape the complications of life where they had previously lived, but also because of hopes for the future. It was suggested that colonists from the Dakotas, Michigan, Wisconsin and Minnesota, in particular, could find homes and work there, and not feel the climate to be too different from that of their home states. In the end, however, the new settlers came from many areas, and wherever unemployment was heavy. It took a few years to turn them into Alaskans, but now, in the third generation, they have become indigenous. Matanuska was perhaps the first colonization to become permanent.

When Ernest Gruening became governor, he advocated a complete modernization of this great state, a total change from territory to statehood. First, he wanted airmail brought to Alaska. Until then, mail had come by ship. Second, he wanted airport development to encourage business and tourism. Third, Alaska had to build international highways connecting her with the other states, and thus remove her isolation. Fourth, parks and accommodations were to be provided for tourists. Fifth, its natural resources were to be developed for a permanent population. Taken together, these recommendations have provided a map for the future of Alaska, a map which has become reality as Alaska has prospered in its livelihood and the enjoyment of life in its magnificent landscape.

What are the people of Alaska today? They are, in the main, descendants of frontiersmen and pioneers. They are individualists who judge men and women not by their social positions but by what they can do in Alaska. They have developed a classless society. Everyone works, and no one is better than any other. They use first names; they are generous in helping each other. They have a trait which we do not associate with frontiersmen, however. They like to read books, and they value education and learning. There are many book buyers and magazine subscribers. Yet pioneering and homesteading continue and will for a long time in the vast area of Alaska. The diversity makes for an interesting life, rich in its contrasts, in this state with its superb scenery.

Scenery! I have heard described more than once the matchless Chitina Valley, the most glorious, perhaps, on our continent. The highest peaks of North America are here, and they are reflected in many clear lakes. Several peaks are above sixteen thousand feet, and they stand in great forests full of game of every kind. The highest is Mount McKinley, twenty thousand, three hundred and twenty feet. Snows are deep in the winter everywhere in Alaska, but they disappear in the summer except on mountain tops. Yes, the natural beauty of Alaska is one of its great resources, too.

ARIZONA

Arizona is a State which I have visited many times for many reasons. It is a place of extremes and contrasts: snow-covered mountains and desert stretches, modern cities and Indian huts, playgrounds of the rich and miners' shacks. It was the youngest of our states until Alaska and Hawaii attained that place, a territory in 1863 and a state in 1912. Its earliest inhabitants were the Indians, followed by Spaniards from Mexico who came in the seventeenth century; Mexicans still come today. Rural villages are many, their inhabitants farmers, still active or retired, religiously narrow and even straitlaced, yet as native to Arizona as cowboys on their bucking broncos.

In the typical Arizonian, if there be such a person at all, is to be discovered a common tendency to brag. True, there is a great deal to brag about. The Grand Canyon, for example, deserves and demands superlatives. I have viewed it many times but only from the air. Coward that I am when it comes to heights, I never expect to see it face to face, so to speak. And the Painted Desert, which I have seen in all its spectacular beauty, who can boast untruthfully about that? Aside from the violent beauty of snowy peaks and flowering deserts, there are the strange saguaro cacti, those vegetable monsters which take the place of trees in their dry and thorny fashion, and which do not reach their full growth until they have lived a hundred years. And the wild horses— who can deny the beauty of a herd of wild horses galloping across the desert in moonlight as bright as an ordinary day, or gathered about a waterhole where the herd has paused to drink? Or who can gainsay the weird beauty of the ancient Petrified Forest?

In resources, Arizona is of course extravagantly rich in minerals. There are enormous reserves in copper and where there is copper there are usually gold, silver and lead. Copper is also a by-product in molybdenum mines, and gold and silver are recovered from lead and zinc ores in more than one mining area.

Arizona's forests, ample in number, are found in the higher altitudes and provide the material for her sawmills. I believe that the largest yellow pine area in the United States is to be found in Arizona. Water is allied to forests anywhere and desert country needs water. The state has provided stores of water in its dams and irrigation projects. I remember the notable Roosevelt Dam, an immense structure two hundred and eighty-four feet high, creating a twenty-five mile reservoir. There are several other large dams, also. Interesting it is to note the many hot springs, significant of earlier volcanic life.

Arizona is, of course, the geologist's delight. The variety and color of her rocks, the story they tell of prehistoric life, are evident even to the untrained eye. I am no geologist, however, and must content myself with the unusual and beautiful flowers and plants of the desert country. If there

are good rains in the winter months, the desert in spring is gorgeous beyond belief. One must see it to know its infinite variety in shape and color, from the snowbank primrose blooming in the snow of the mountains near Flagstaff, altitude higher than twelve thousand feet, to the acres of yellow poppies in the lowlands along highways flanked by myriads of other flowers. I am especially fond of the yucca with its stalk of cream-white bells rising from its dagger leaves of dark green. Then there is the night-blooming cereus, the queen of flowers, which once a year blooms through a night in June and dies at dawn. How

often I have sat through a night, sleepless, to watch the solemnly beautiful spectacle.

I confess I am less fond of the wild animal life of Arizona. Snakes abound; only in India have I felt it so necessary to be aware of their presence. Cobras in India and rattlesnakes in Arizona— reluctantly I grant their bizarre beauty but let it be far away from me. The king snake, I am told, is harmless, and immune to rattlesnake venom. It consequently attacks and even eats them, for which I am grateful, though it seems grim fare. Lizards, too, abound; while they have been defended in my presence as harmless, I do not care for their snaky looks, particularly the variety which runs on its hind legs when frightened, a sight that is horridly human.

Let us think rather of birds, of which there are some four hundred varieties in Arizona; a hundred and fifty or so are permanent residents, the others visitors at various seasons for various lengths of time. There are even parrots, large and with thick beaks, a tropical species, although eagles and falcons are also to be found. But then Arizona once had camels, imported before the days of the railroads, and it is said they carried their heavy burdens across the deserts with ease.

As for the people of Arizona, they too are various, both good and bad, of many origins and species. They are as they may be, and can be as exciting or as notable as the gorgeous, glorious, magnificent land which by the accident of fate has been given to them.

ARKANSAS

Arkansas is a State of which I knew too little for a long time. True, coming and going westward, I always looked forward to the beautiful Ozark Mountains—hills, they seemed, after the violence of the Rocky Mountains—and I enjoyed their tender green slopes and the quiet Arkansas River. There are whole areas of forest in Arkansas that look, I read, much as they did when Hernando de Soto looked upon them in 1541. So enamored did I become with the Ozarks that once I took a young man, imaginary, from those mountains to be a character in a novel of mine. There is, of course, also the Ouachita Range, separated from the Ozarks by the Arkansas River.

As to Arkansas itself, it seems that it produces more barite than any other state in our Union. I did not know what barite was when this information was given me and upon inquiry I learned it is something used in the making of rubber, paper and other products. Arkansas is the only place in North America, too, to have diamond mines, but they are not workable for reasons I could not discover. Oil is found and produced, however, in sizable quantities, as it is in so many of our states, leading me to wonder sometimes if our entire country floats upon a sea of oil.

As in other states, in Arkansas, the French came after the Spaniards, and rough log cabins soon clustered into settlements. The Louisiana Purchase made it all the territory of the United States in 1803, however. Now the state is a source of fine timber, many varieties of delicious fruits and vegetables and that sour sweet, called sorghum. The state has still an atmosphere of rugged youth, it seems to me, and it will develop with time, I am sure, into one of our most valuable areas. Not all its treasures are yet revealed.

The Arkansas Post National Memorial is interesting because it marks the first permanent white settlement west of the Mississippi River, not counting Spanish settlements in the Southwest. The French colony was set up by Henri de Tonti, a lieutenant to La Salle. For a hundred and twenty years it was a point of contest and struggle for the whole Mississippi Valley, but French soldiers continued to hold it. In 1719 and 1720 an ambitious man, John Law, planned to make himself a duke of the area; he issued unsecured paper currency and brought in the first slaves. The "Mississippi Bubble," as it was called, burst of its own weight, and in 1819, the settlement became the capital of Arkansas Territory. Arkansas' first newspaper, *The Arkansas Gazette*, was published there. Later, in 1821, both capital and newspaper were moved to Little Rock and there they have stayed. Arkansas became a state on June 15, 1836, and it was our twenty-fifth state. It was and is called the Land of Opportunity, which implies, I think, its youth and potential.

Speaking of the Ozarks, there is a pleasant little resort town there called Eureka Springs. Its streets climb up and down and around until one foot can scarcely follow the other. Most remarkable, however, are the springs, sixty-three of them to be exact, which flow from the limestone in clear abundance. One can enter caves even from the main street. On Magnetic Mountain, a seven-story high statue, Christ of the Ozarks, stands gazing over the town. The people here like to call their area the Switzerland of America, with some truth, it can be said.

Fayetteville is another delightful resort town, and the University of Arkansas is here, which centers my interest. Fort Smith is the home of the Fort Smith Historical Site, a restoration of a period of law enforced by that doughty old character, Judge Isaac C. Parker. The circumstances are as follows: Fort Smith had been built in 1817 to keep the Osage Indians up the Arkansas River and the Cherokee Indians down the river, and also as a protection for traders, explorers and others. Captain John Rogers led the first settlement there in 1821, and others followed until it was a sizable small town. In 1848, however, gold was discovered and a crowd rushed in, reputable and disreputable. There was no law, no order, until in 1875 Judge Parker moved in and restored both by hanging those who broke the laws and created disorder, hanging on one occasion as many as six men in one day. He lived there for twenty-one years, feared but at the same time respected for his justice. During all those years he held court every day except Sundays and Christmas. I wonder that no one has written his story. Perhaps it has been and I have not found it.

Arkansas has only one outlet to the sea and it is Helena, a river barge port-of-call. I am told that in 1880 Mark Twain avowed it was set on the loveliest spot on the Mississippi. Perhaps he passed it sometimes. The town stands in what is called cotton country, in the rich delta region of the Mississippi Valley.

The Hot Springs National Park deserves mention before we leave Arkansas. About a million gallons a day of hot, mineral water flow from these springs, of which there are forty-seven. The water is distributed to various bathhouses, all under the administration of the Federal government, and the medicinal use of the water is under the supervision of the Libby Memorial Physical Medical Center. Visitors come from all over the world to enjoy the baths and to seek medical cures. The city of Hot Springs itself, is more than a spa, however. It is a place to enjoy for its modern accommodations and the lovely natural scenery of the Ouachita Hills.

Little Rock, the capital of Arkansas, is well known to the country, and indeed to the world, for reasons sometimes distressful, its racial troubles. Those times now are past, hopefully, and I prefer to think of it as the City of Roses, for the climate seems to encourage these, my favorite flower; roses are everywhere. There is a legend about its name. It is said that a French explorer, Bernard de la Harpe, heard that there was a huge rock in this area composed entirely of emerald. Here he came searching in 1722, to find only a huge rock but not of emerald. He called it Big Rock and downstream discovered a smaller one which he called Little Rock. Big or little, he was not a man of much imagination, it seems.

In conclusion, I suggest once more that Arkansas is still in a period of growth and development and there is much more to be discovered there in years to come.

CALIFORNIA

Of all our American states, this long narrow State lying between sea and mountains has the greatest variety in climate, landscape and history. There is more than just a touch of Spain here, its influence to be seen in the ancient buildings of the Spanish

missionaries. They left more than the missions which today are visited by thousands of tourists. They left the aura of dignity, even greatness, for they were men of culture and spiritual grace. California more than any other state, with the possible exception of Louisiana, seems to hang like a lovely fruit between old Europe and the New World. There is a sense of history in California, not of its own, but of its founders.

I always visit the missions, for I miss in this young country of ours the presence of past centuries. How often have I lingered in San Juan Capistrano, for example! The swallows still come back on the appointed day, I am told, but our arrival never coincides. And somehow, lingering there, I catch faint memories of Asia. The Spanish Franciscan fathers visited the Philippines long ago and left behind them similar white monasteries among the same kinds of bright tropical flowers and trees.

In San Francisco there is the best Chinese settlement in the Western world. The Chinese there know me and press gifts upon me from their shops. The restaurants serve me their best secret dainties, not offered to the usual traveler, and I have gifts of jade and ivory from dealers in antiques. My favorite goddess, a Kuanyin centuries old and carved in fragrant camphorwood, I was given in a huge dark and dusty shop, with whose owner I talked in our native Mandarin Chinese throughout an autumn afternoon. We exchanged

our memories. His home had been in Peking and it was there he had found my Goddess of Mercy. She stands now beside an old hand-hewn pillar in my Vermont home; the pedestal upon which she stands is an ancient root of polished blackwood which we bought once upon a time in Korea.

As for the people in California, they are samples of all our people. They come from every state to enjoy climate and scene—a perilous enjoyment, for the foundations of the state, which hangs between sea and mountain ranges, are un-

steady. The people know this, but golden California charms them into ignoring what may happen, what must happen if we are to believe what seismologists tell us. Yet all human beings know their certain end and ignore it, enjoying life from day to day as each tomorrow becomes today.

An assorted people, nevertheless, are these people of California! All parts of the world have contributed to the variety. The Chinese are, for the most part, the descendants of the South Chinese laborers who came to work on the railroad at the time of the Gold Rush. Japanese farmers and gardeners settled, before World War II, in the areas around Los Angeles and south. Mexicans flooded into the Imperial Valley, and Filipinos into many towns and villages. Winemaking drew Italians and Armenians to vineyards, and dairy farms attracted the Portuguese. Scandinavians went to lumbering and black Americans to jobs in city hotels. People from every European country, Russia included, came to visit beautiful California and stayed to live there. The variety of the people is only matched by the variety of the landscape from seashore to high mountains, from desert to forest.

It is no wonder, I have come to see, that the United States sometimes finds it difficult to remain united. Each state functions as a nation in itself; each citizen may believe that his state is the best in the country and therefore his first loyalty, unexpressed or proclaimed, is to his state. We are nevertheless a nation and as a nation we take our place in the world of nations. We are a family of states, and like brothers and sisters we quarrel among ourselves, but in times of peril we present a solid front.

I come away from California with rich memories of beauty. I should be hard put to it if I had to choose among them. Yet the most awesome are the hours I have spent in the forests of giant redwoods, which are the sole survivors on earth of trees extinct since the Ice Age.

46

COLORADO

I approached Denver in silence. Our car had been steadily climbing the rising land. Suddenly we were in Denver. It struck me immediately with its stunning beauty. The sky was a cloudless blue. The air was pure and exhilarating. The handsome modern city was clean and well planned, its lines straight and uncrowded. The people were pleasant, friendly and relaxed. They were not cowboys, and they did not even appear to belong to the cowboy period. They were modern businessmen and smart, modern women. Even the children seemed happy and relaxed. It must be, I thought, the high, pure air. It must be the unclouded sky. More than three hundred days a year the sun shines, I was told. It is not a large city, this Denver. It has more than a million people, to be sure, but it is not crowded. There is room for a hundred named parks, for tennis courts and swimming pools, flower beds and lawns. Nearby in the mountains are huge national parks.

There is an air of youthfulness about Denver and, indeed, about the State of Colorado itself. The landscapes are bold. I do not know its geologic age, but it has a newly hewn look; the mountains are high, some of them forever snow capped, the canyons deep, the rivers swift. Early Indians lived in cliff dwellings once on the Mesa Verde, a vast green flat, fifty thousand acres of mesa and canyons. For some reason still unknown, these Indians left the area suddenly but not before they had begun to build the Sun Temple, which they did not finish.

The Garden of the Gods; the many ghost towns, some of them now being revived; the mountain peaks, six hundred of them more than twelve thousand feet high, three hundred more than thirteen thousand feet and fifty-two more than fourteen thousand, compel the traveler to awe. The gorges are deeper, the rivers run more swiftly, the people are more genial and open hearted here than elsewhere, or so it seems.

On Lookout Mountain is the tomb of Buffalo Bill Cody, that figure loved, admired and finally debunked. Yet no debunking can totally destroy the symbol of the West somehow contained within his being. This is an argument strangely personal to me, for my husband himself in his youth had written a book debunking the legendary figure, only to find that readers refused to accept the truth about the man.

As for me, I love the mining ghost towns of Colorado and especially I love the old Victorian houses—Healy House in Leadville and Maxwell House in Georgetown, early silver and gold mining centers. Leadville is a remarkable place. It sits at an altitude of more than ten thousand

feet, and its air of former grace still remains in the Tabor Opera House and the Vendome Hotel. The Climax Molybdenum Mine, which supplies three-fifths of the world's molybdenum, is near Leadville.

The Great Plains are in northern Colorado. Once they were endless seas of waving grass, and prairie schooners traveled westward on what was called the Starvation Trail. Stories of cannibalism still linger in old men's tales. Now, however, fine

farms enrich the soil and yield their treasure, thanks to irrigation canals. Yet the past is not so far away, for there are still buffalo ruts and wallows to be seen.

Pikes Peak was the goal of many early settlers in their search for gold, and Colorado Springs grew out of that impetuous search. The city is said to be one of the most beautiful in the country, a modern city, where sophisticated visitors linger to become residents. Pueblo, I am told, still retains much of the scenery and spirit of the early West.

Colorado slants upward to the Continental Divide and breaks into the glorious mountains which moved Katherine M. Bates to write "America the Beautiful." Southeastern Colorado is watered by the Arkansas River. It was along this river that the Santa Fe Trail wended its way, a path for traders and explorers, soldiers and Indians into Colorado. There are many interesting towns and monuments along this route. I think especially of Trinidad with its old trading post. A fine specimen of Victorian architecture is the mansion of the pioneer merchant, Frank Bloom. It is now a museum, as is the trading post, and there is a fine rose garden surrounding the Bloom mansion.

In these modern days, Colorado is famous for its skiing resorts. Sunshine and dry powdery snow, restaurants and inns provide exercise and amusement for thousands of people from November until May. The citizens of Colorado everywhere are friendly and good humored. There is an atmosphere prevalent of confidence and youth which is most refreshing, especially to those who live in the crowded cities of the East.

Summing it up, it seems to me that Colorado expresses the best of the West. The privations of pioneer days are over. The advantages of modern life are taken as a matter of course. It is a pleasant stage.

CONNECTICUT

This State I cross again and again, each time pausing to look at some portly building facing the sea, or some handsome house. It is interesting to realize the human changes that have taken place here in the years since 1630, when settlers began to move in from Massachusetts. The colonists were English for the most part, although a Dutchman, Adriaen Block, had been perhaps the first explorer to arrive. Coasting along the shoreline and entering the Connecticut River in 1614, he observed the possibilities of the green countryside, inhabited then only by the wandering Indians. Even the Dutch did not settle there for twenty years, however, and it was in 1632 that an Englishman, Edward Winslow, hearing good reports from Indians, visited the Connecticut Valley. From then on the influx of people was mainly English and so it continued through the Revolutionary War, until the middle of the nineteenth century when immigration was mainly from Europe. Meanwhile, many of the younger English had emigrated, why one can only surmise. Apparently it was the wandering instinct of youth, seeking greener pastures and wider lands of their own. It is true, however, that the rocky glacial soil of Connecticut has not lent itself easily to productive farming, the occupation of the early settlers.

In the succeeding years since, Connecticut has become an industrialized area. The European immigrants provided cheap labor, and specialized industries peculiar to localities have developed. Insurance companies today predominate.

Of course, where there are many manufacturers, particularly perhaps many small ones as in Connecticut, there are also sure to be strikes and labor unrest. For the last century and a half this has been true in the state. Workers have

become increasingly aware of their rights to be independent and to attain some sort of economic and social freedom in accordance with modern times. This determination has been true of farmers as well, especially since the increase of residential areas condemns them to small farms, too small, often, to make the necessary capital investment in farm machinery possible or practical.

With all this change, however, the state has preserved its individual flavor and atmosphere to a surprising extent, considering the variety of religions, occupations and origins of its citizens. It is a small state, one of the original thirteen, only Delaware and Rhode Island being smaller. The countryside always makes me think of England, its rolling hills and wide green valleys so like the English lowlands. It has only one real mountain, Bear Mountain, which is just two thousand, three hundred and fifty-five feet high. But height is relative and it dominates its area. The Berkshire Hills are beautiful, and the Litchfield and Norfolk Hills provide pleasant areas for campers and summer people, and ski areas for winter visitors.

The historic old houses of Connecticut are rich in stories, and many of them are handsome in the English colonial style. They have been restored and are inhabited today by people of wealth, many of whom have businesses in New York. Indeed, the commuting distances are very short, one point over the Penn-Central Railroad being only twelve miles from New Haven to the state line of Connecticut. It is a pleasant journey, too, by car along the beautifully designed parkways that connect it to New York and to many points in New England.

The people of Connecticut today are, as far as I have known them, conservative in temperament. Law and order are respected and on the whole observed. The atmosphere is quiet and peaceful. For many decades, the local governments contrived to function according to the state constitution of 1818. But the many amendments, more than forty, show a disposition to change, even to modernize, but along lines defined by the Constitution of the United States.

Nowhere has this trend been more evident than in anti-pollution efforts, in which fisheries have hastened to be active. Commercial fishing has always been important in Connecticut. Oyster farming, for example, can yield well over a thou-

sand dollars an acre. It was in Connecticut that I first even heard of oyster farming going on in this country, although I knew very well and had seen for myself the pearl-oyster farming of Japan.

Family wise, for the average citizen, Connecticut is an attractive state because of its excellent school system. Good education has been a concern from the beginning, when Puritan forebears in church and life encouraged good schools. At first these schools were privately founded and owned, but a century or so ago public schools were established and of course have continued. There are also a certain number of fashionable finishing schools for "young ladies." I suppose proximity to the society circles in New York keeps the schools prosperous. The most famous university is of course Yale. When its establishment was first contemplated, there were objections that nearby Harvard could supply all the educational needs of young men in New England and environs. This caused no more than delay, however, and in 1701 the Connecticut General Assembly decided to set up the college. In 1713, Elihu Yale, a wealthy resident of London who had been born in the United States, gave something over seven hundred pounds to the college, whereupon it was decided to name the school for him. He had grown rich, by the way, as the governor of Madras, India. There are many other fine schools in Connecticut, too many to mention, although none perhaps is as well known as Yale. A fine and very old Federal land-grant college, Connecticut College, provides excellent education in agriculture.

All in all, Connecticut is one of our more mature and sophisticated states. The roughness of pioneer days has long been smoothed away by time, by experience and by proximity to great cities, which are in themselves centers of culture and arts supported by flourishing industry. Its well-groomed rural life keeps it from becoming a suburb of these cities, however, and thus helps to maintain its identity.

DELAWARE

Delaware is the second smallest of the fifty states which comprise the United States of America. Its area is only two thousand, three hundred and ninety-nine miles. Yet it is a notable State for its past history, its present wealth and the pride of its people. Much of its flourishing industry is built on the energy and ability of the DuPont family, whose fortune was founded on gunpowder.

The people of Delaware are of a mixed origin, Scandinavian, English, French, Scotch, Irish and Dutch. These have been independent folk, and the citizens of Delaware today are fiercely independent. This perhaps is partly because of the small size of the state. It contains only three counties, a hundred and ten miles altogether in length, and is nine miles wide at its narrowest point and thirty-five miles at its widest.

Wilmington is of course its capital and its largest city, as well as the center of its industry. Nearby is Winterthur, the great DuPont mansion that is now a museum of American antiques. The vast gardens surrounding the house are a famous sight, especially in the spring. Dover and Newcastle are also unique towns, because of their attractive colonial style houses, which provide an atmosphere of elegance.

Small as Delaware is, it contains, nevertheless, a combination of landscape and industry. More than half of its acreage, except for the marshes along the coast, is used for poultry and dairy farming, and for growing soybeans, tomatoes, corn, asparagus and fruit. The strawberries are especially fine. Northern and central Delaware are flourishing centers of industries. In addition to all this, Delaware is known as the Corporation Center of the world. This is because its state corporation policies have attracted so many business firms to incorporate under its aegis.

Delaware's scenery is varied. Lovely, forested hills lift their heads in the northern section. These change to sand dunes in the south and to long stretches of unvarying marshes along the coast. The coastland has been the source of many legends of sunken ships full of treasure. A ship foundered there as early as 1798, and much searching has taken place since then, for it was said that it was loaded with gold coin and bullion. It is true that occasionally coins do wash ashore on Coin Beach near the town of Rehobeth.

The state itself was named for Lord de la Warr, the governor of Virginia. Its history began with the arrival of twenty-eight Dutchmen who settled on its shores in 1631. A year later, in a quarrel with Indians, all of them were murdered, their fields burned and their cattle killed. In 1638, a colony of Swedes was established near what is now Wilmington. Dutch, French, English, Irish and Scotch came after them, and later still these were followed by German, Polish and Italian immigrants.

Delaware was the first state to adopt the Constitution of the United States. The memorable date is December 7, 1787. It has been a proudly independent state ever since. It has had its distinguished citizens. Among these were two whom I knew, Henry Seidel Canby, literary critic and long editor of *The Saturday Review of Literature,* whose shy and charming wife was a gifted and too little appreciated poet, and John P. Marquand, the well-known and very successful novelist.

New Castle is perhaps one of the most historic and certainly one of the most delightful of Delaware's towns. It was the first one to be planned. It was the first capital of the state; here the

colonial assemblies took place, and culture has always been its atmosphere. Three signers of the Declaration of Independence lived in New Castle—Thomas McKean, George Ross, Jr. and George Read. The town has an excellent harbor and for long was a thriving port, until Wilmington's nearness to Philadelphia gave that Delaware city the advantage.

The town of Odessa is interesting because for years before the Civil War it was an important station in the Underground Railroad. Rehobeth Beach is a curiosity as well as a fine beach resort. It has sometimes been called the nation's Summer Capital because it is so convenient to Washington, and the government officials and members of the diplomatic corps. All the usual sports and seaside occupations are to be enjoyed there, including a seashore state park and golfing. Delaware has named sundry towns after foreign cities—Odessa, after the port on the Black Sea through which Russia ships out grain, and Smyrna, after the chief seaport in Turkey.

Wilmington is of course the hub of Delaware. It is called the Chemical Capital of the World. It was first settled by Swedes and Finns brought there by Peter Minuit, a Dutchman. The Dutch, under peg-legged Peter Stuyvesant, Governor of New Netherland, took it over in 1655. In 1664, the English took control through wealthy Quakers. Under their canny leadership, it became a prosperous industrial center.

I travel often to and fro across this small, contented state, which apparently lives in peace with itself and with the world.

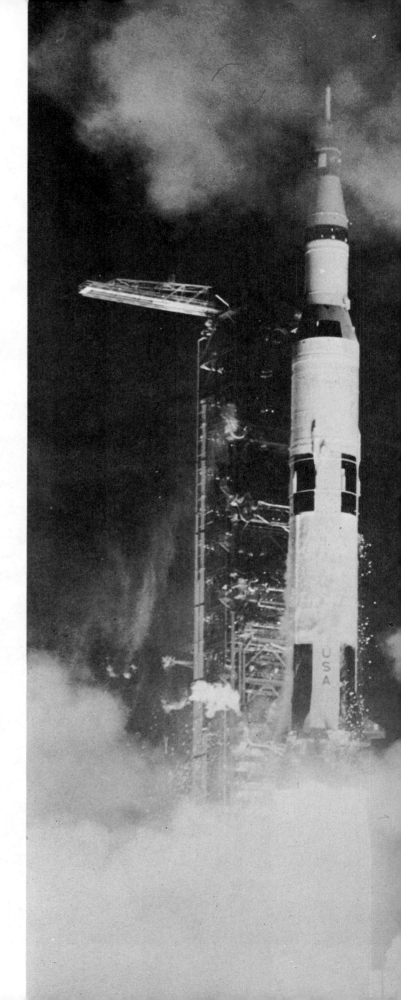

FLORIDA

Florida, I have read, is the oldest State in our history but the youngest in its development. I doubt the last half of the sentence. It is more than four hundred years old in western terms, and in some ways antediluvian in its vegetable and animal life. A slow journey by houseboat through the Everglades is a fascinating and in some ways an eerie experience. The monster alligators, which look and behave like crocodiles, are representative enough of an earlier age to frighten the casual observer into the dim and terrifying past when monsters came up out of murky waters.

As a matter of fact, Florida has a longer coastline than that of any other of our states, it has jungles and pine-covered hills, it has rolling hills and valleys of farmland. It has everything except snow-topped mountains. All of it, however, is lowlying. If I remember my statistics correctly, it nowhere reaches five hundred feet above sea level. The soil is sand, but not like the fine sand of northern states. Much, though not all, of Florida's sand, fine white stuff that it is, is made of pulverized bones or shells, or crusts of coral and other sea creatures. It forms a solid base for Florida's many buildings.

The lushness of Florida's vegetation is of course due to its rainfall, which is usually about fifty-seven inches a year. This, and the sea breezes, keep the state endurably cool. There is so much water everywhere, however, that some trees, such as the cypress, have learned to grow in water. Cypress, incidentally, is a lovely wood and makes fine furniture, although it has to be seasoned in the air and not in kilns. I do not know why this is

except that, contrary to pine, cypress needs a long time to dry out. Pine, also an ample Florida crop, can be dried in kilns but it is a quickly growing tree compared to cypress; a cypress takes as much as two hundred years, I understand, to grow into lumber size.

Florida astonished me with its agriculture. However this may be, one thinks of it as a place for fun and enjoyment by the rich and poor. This is exemplified in the mansions of the rich in Palm Beach and in my memory when, years ago, a young maid servant I had in my Pennsylvania house gave notice.

"Because, madame," she said, "my father-in-

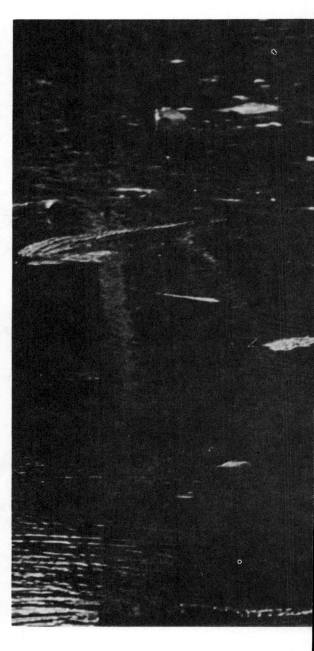

law has gone on relief and he's takin' us for a vacation in Florida."

What other attractions has Florida? Many, I am sure, for all those people who look on it as heaven and haven. I, who love flowers, consider it the land of flowers. So, apparently, do others for as long ago as more than half a century, a great garden of flowers was growing there for the making of perfumes and fragrant oils. Then, of course, there are the orange groves with their fragrant orange blossoms, and the grapefruit and lemon. Florida needs no greenhouses. The mild air grows every kind of flower. Wandering about one day in such a garden at Silver Springs, we came upon a green parrot for sale. He greeted us with such vivacity in both English and Spanish—and, it must be confessed, Sailor—that we bought him on the spot and he has been part of our household ever since. A Korean houseboy added his language to the parrot's accomplishments.

There are curious and strange acts of nature in beautiful Florida. I was intrigued, for example, by stories of the disappearance and reappearance of lakes. Lake Neff, for one, has vanished and appeared again several times, I am told. The explanation seems to be in the subsoil of Florida which rests upon a deep layer of limestone. When a break occurs in this foundation, water drains away for a time. When the break is filled up in time with the refuse of nature, water collects again and the lake once more seems to appear.

Like every other state, Florida has its lapses from beauty. There are flat areas in the south that seem to grow only scrubby pines and useless vegetation. I ignore such areas and concentrate only on gardens and beaches, orange and lemon groves, and the chain of exquisite islets called the Keys. When I think of animal life there, I take for granted the many more or less common varieties of birds, and remember instead the great white heron—dying out, also—the egrets and the matchless grace and dignity of the brilliant flamingoes.

As for the people of Florida, they have come from every state and clime and, as I have said, from the rich and the poor. But the base is a mixture of so-called cracker, or the pioneer who was usually a white man, the Latin-American, Negro and Seminole Indian—all making together a heady American brew!

GEORGIA

When I think of the State of Georgia, I seem to breathe again its strange, dying odor. When that sweetish stink first rose to my nostrils I inquired of its origin, suspecting dead fish, rotting swamps, receding tides, burning garbage, stale cape jessamine; I was told that it was the paper mills. I believe firmly that it is a compound of all these sources. Whatever it is, it is ever present and most so in the beautiful old city of Savannah—beautiful with parks and houses, a fine seaport—a lovely place to visit in spite of its atmosphere.

Georgia's trees are hung with sad gray Spanish moss. There are those persons who love Spanish moss but I am not one of them. It makes me think of old rags, spiders' webs in deserted houses and vultures hanging like dirty bags in the trees of India. Somehow one suspects the moss of contributing evil to the atmosphere, not true of course. I am told it does not kill the trees, this Spanish moss. My only reply to that is to ask why so many trees that are draped with it are dead? There is never an answer to this except the insistence that they are not dead, in spite of being leafless.

Georgia's blacks are Gullahs. They are smoothly dark, fine featured and small boned. They came originally from West Africa, a silent, withdrawn people, thinking their own thoughts. They seem to belong in Georgia, especially in the extraordinary region of the Okefenokee Swamp.

This area of brown water lakes, strange moss, huge cypress trees and creeping animals, birds and beasts, is in fact a vast marsh. In spring, it is gorgeous with flowers, but the earth quivers under one's feet.

Atlanta, now, is another story. Sometimes I believe that Georgia has never recovered from the memory of Sherman's devastating march. Only in Atlanta do I feel a total recovery. It is a fine modern city, linked in my memory with members

of my father's family, an uncle, handsome and distinguished; his wife, the first woman in the United States to win a PhD; their son, my first cousin, a famous physician whom the whole state held in honor. Atlanta was destroyed in the Civil War and built again. Perhaps in the rebuilding, the old pain was washed away.

There are many pleasant memories connected with this state, especially for anyone with a love of history. The first permanent settlement in Georgia was founded by James Oglethorpe, on behalf of a group of English colonists. It was named for King George II of England. Their efforts settled the struggles of over two hundred years among Spain, France and England for domination of the area. The Indians were gradually driven away to other lands and English builders and artisans were brought in. Today it is a populous and busy state.

Georgia peaches! They come to mind, delectable and delicious. But not only peaches grow well there. It produces peanuts and cotton, has truck gardening, beef and dairy cattle. The cotton gin was invented here by Eli Whitney in 1793. From here, too, the first steamship, *The Savannah,* crossed the ocean in 1819, and again in 1963, another *Savannah* was the first nuclear-powered American merchant ship. There was another *first* in an entirely different field—the first use of ether as an anaesthetic, by a Georgia surgeon in 1842 named Crawford W. Long.

There are many interesting historical places in Georgia for her history is exciting. Cottage Colony and the Jekyll Island Club of sixty millionaires are owned now by the state. President Franklin D. Roosevelt's Little White House is at Warm Springs. The great pre-historic mounds of Indian origin are in Georgia as well as elsewhere. The largest brick fort in the world is near Savannah, and at Andersonville is the former Confederate prison of evil memory. This military prison was built in 1863–1864 to house originally ten thousand men and actually held thirty-three thousand. The death rate was shockingly high due to overcrowding, miserable food, a shortage of medicines and medical attention and, perhaps, to the refusal of the North to exchange prisoners. Fifteen thousand soldiers' graves are in the Andersonville National Cemetery. Providence Spring is here, and legend has it that the spring burst out of sandy soil after a sudden rain following the drought in the summer of 1864.

Augusta comes to mind as an interesting town because of its firsts, also. The first steamboat in southern waters was launched here. *The Augusta Chronicle* and *The Herald*, begun in 1785, are the South's oldest continuous newspapers, and the state's first medical academy was chartered here in 1828. The academy, now the Medical College of Georgia, is especially famous for its distinguished research in cardiovascular and cardiopulmonary physiology.

Indian Spring State Park is said to be the oldest state park in the United States. The mineral spring there was used by the Indians for medicinal purposes.

It is an old and lovely state that we have.

HAWAII

Hawaii, our newest State, is not as distant from the mainland as it may appear. It used to seem very far away when I was a small girl traveling with my parents by steamship across the Pacific Ocean long ago. It is in fact something over two thousand miles from San Francisco, nearer than the latter is from Washington, D.C. or New York. Today, in a few hours, we mainlanders can reach Honolulu, the capital, by air.

How many happy visits I have spent in that lovely city, hanging like a jewel or like a basket of flowers, to the cliff-like mountains towering above it! The whole picture is striking and brilliant— the glittering blue sea, the rushing white surf, the colorful buildings and the high mountains with their deep dark valleys, those montains whose heights seem always to be hooded in black clouds. Nowadays there is a parallel with that darkness hovering above the sunlit city and the bright sea. The parallel shadow is a memory that cannot be forgotten because it is there. I never drive past the harbor without remembering that at its bottom the battleship *Arizona* lies mortally wounded, in her silent hulk rest more than a thousand young American men who hurried to their death on the day when Pearl Harbor was attacked.

The memory remains but the sun still shines on Hawaii. The rains fall suddenly, at any hour of

the day or night, and the sea can foam into un-
expected storm but the sun still shines on Hawaii.
It is a happy place in spite of past sorrow, a place
where exotic flowers bloom eternally, where fruits
are sweet, and there is neither heat nor cold. The
people are a happy people, a mixture of many
races and nations living together in mutual acceptance and content. Life seems relaxed and
easy, yet I know those magnificent fields of sugar
cane and pineapple are the result of human hands
hard at work.

Reflecting upon this atmosphere of peace and
absence of tension, I wonder if it does not owe a
debt to the spirit of the Christian missionaries who
went there long ago? I know great fun was made
about those puritan New Englanders with their
long skirts and frock coats, but it must be remembered that they were abolitionists, against
slavery, and they honestly believed that all people
were alike, that all were the children of God.
Today in the fragrant air of Hawaii one feels that
same spirit. The people are all the children of
God, and they have gathered there from everywhere, black and white, yellow and brown, all,
equal in opportunity. In such ways, Hawaii is the
most ideally American of all our states for its
people are truly united.

Honolulu, the main city, is on the large island
of Oahu. There are other islands which I have
not visited yet, less developed materially, and one
may reach them by air. Each time I go to Oahu I
plan to visit the other islands and do not, beacause
this is too pleasant a place to leave, the air sweetly
languorous, the sky so blue in spite of a drifting
cloud, a sudden spatter of silvery rain. My routine
is simple. When I have rested for a day, I take the
drive around the island, but not quite completely
around, for at the island's far end the cliffs are so
abrupt that the roads wash away. Somewhere, I
stop to visit the Dole pineapple plantations.
There, in the midst of the fields, is an open
building where one can sit and eat a ripe pine-

78

apple that has been cut into slices and chilled. The
sweetness of this sun-ripened fruit is so enticing,
so satisfying that I eat a whole pineapple, un-
thinkable anywhere else in the world. Then I go
on my way.

The sunshine, the sea, the sudden showers are
all so dramatic, so enchanting, that they almost
make me ignore, or fail to note, what is really
most remarkable about this American state: it is
of course the people, so subtly blended by life together that they present a foretaste of the future
of the human race, when we have all learned to
live together in peace. They are the most beautiful
people in the world, uniting all races into one.
There are Hawaiians who boast that their grand-
parents came from four different countries, east
and west. It is fascinating to study Hawaiian faces
and see the blends and note which strains predominate—Polynesian, Asian, European, African.

What else? Ah yes, Honolulu itself has all the
American adjuncts, movies, hotels, apartment
houses, restaurants, shops and museums, and always superb swimming and fishing. I have never
tried the latter. When evening comes I go out on
the wide terrace of my hotel apartment and,
stretched out on a long chair, a tall cool pineapple
drink on the table at my side, I watch the moon
rise over Diamond Head.

IDAHO

Idaho is a study in contrasts. This variety in landscape and climate is true, I find, in most of our states, except those that are predominantly desert. I wonder, therefore, if the contrasts to which our people are born and in which they are nurtured, does not account for, in some measure at least, the mercurial character of Americans. Generally speaking, we are subject to instant temperamental

changes. We can be open, cheerful, generous beyond need or expectation. In an instant, at a word, we can be murderously violent.

Be this as it may, Idaho, to an amazing degree, provides the background of contrast. It is volcanic even in its origin, as by and large is our whole country, with extensive lava fields. Volcano and glacier shaped the State of Idaho, and melting ice and remnant lakes still feed its rivers. There are also those strange, barren and rocky deserts ap-

propriately called Craters of the Moon. Yet the surrounding countryside of Boise Valley, peaceful and rich, reminds me of the farmlands of Pennsylvania. And even Boise is near the Salmon River Mountains.

I am reminded here that Ernest Hemingway, that turbulent, talented man, so loved the state of Idaho that after his tragic and violent death his body was brought to Idaho for final rest. His grave is in beautiful Sun Valley, looking toward the

Sawtooth Mountains.

What are my own associations with Idaho? My goal, for various reasons, has usually been Boise. It is the capital, of course, and is now the largest city in the state. Before Boise became the capital in 1864, however, Idaho City had been larger. I remember the many trees, Idaho is heavily forested still, and the name of its capital is derived from the French word for forest, *les bois*. The city is a commercial center with ample hydroelectric power for manufacturing. I recall it mainly as a city of astute though friendly businessmen who were not inclined to part too readily with their earnings, even for the best of human causes. The city itself is pleasant. There are parks, a state historical museum, a fine art gallery where I was pleased to find some good oriental art alongside the American and European showings. Another surprise was to find a number of Basques in the city and its environs, making up the largest Basque colony in North America, as a matter of fact. They hold a Basque Festival every summer to add to the variety of Idaho.

I was interested in the town of Blackfoot when I was last in Idaho, because there is an atomic reactor near there. The community was large enough to assemble the required labor to bring consequent prosperity. The town was at first named Grave City at a time when a large group of people detrained there on Christmas Eve, in 1878. I do not know this story or why the name was changed, nor have I been able to find anyone to tell me. Potatoes are an important product in Blackfoot.

I ought to append to the fact about the atomic reactor that the abundance of electric power in the state generally and in its many remote areas has resulted in the decision of the Atomic Energy Commission to build more experimental nuclear reactors here than in any other state. Whatever the feeling of the people may be, they benefit from the jobs that are being created as a consequence.

What else? I have looked down the deepest canyon in North America, Hell's Canyon, nearly eight thousand feet deep. It is here in Idaho. I was told that the largest forest of white pine in the world is in the St. Joe National Forest. Since Idaho is largely agricultural, it has more irrigated acres than any other state. The chief crops are potatoes, fruit, beets and hay as well as livestock. Tourism is another resource. The spectacular scenery of Idaho; the hunting and fishing; the interesting ghost towns, relics of early silver-mining days; the frightening but exciting boat rides on the rough waters of the Salmon River, known once as the River of No Return; Sun Valley and all its modern pleasures—all these invite the tourist. As to parks, about three-fourths of Idaho's land is publicly owned.

Speaking of ghost towns and mining, Idaho still produces more zinc, pumice, antimony and silver than any other state, and only Missouri surpasses it in production of lead. A long list of other minerals are found in Idaho and, liking jewelry, I am glad to report that a number of fine gems are also to be found. I liked especially the opals, rubies and sapphires, but agate, jasper, onyx and garnets are of good quality.

Reflecting upon what I have written here about Idaho, I find my memory returning especially to Craters of the Moon. It is aptly named, this national monument, for its landscape was formed very much as we have been told the moonscape was formed. Within this eighty-three acre tract, a weak spot on the earth's surface allowed eruptions of lava to escape, probably three times, from the earth's interior. The extraordinary shapes of the hardened lava look very much as the surface of the moon appears. The Crater of the Moon is an eerie spot.

Each state exerts its own fascination, but among them all, Idaho is one of the most fascinating in the extraordinary beauty and variety of its landscape.

ILLINOIS

Among all the different states of America, Illinois is in some ways the richest and the most central. As a child, while traveling to and from China with my parents, I remember inquiring of my elders why it was, no matter what our destination,

we always had to go to Chicago first. My father had replied, somewhat grimly, that he had often asked that question of himself but had never found an answer. In those days all through trains went to Chicago first and then scattered in all directions. Today, however, the question still remains, though in modern form, for now through jets go to Chicago first. So, I suppose, Chicago is the answer and in a sense Illinois is the background for Chicago, the second largest city in our nation.

The State of Illinois provides a rich and diverse background for Chicago, nevertheless, a complex of highly productive agriculture and industry. All this power and plenty have developed in the last century and a quarter. Before then the area had been part of territory belonging to the Louisiana Purchase. The name Illinois comes from the Indian tribe, the Illini, meaning "the men." The French version was the influence, I suppose, of the coming of missionaries and explorers in 1673, when Father Jacques Marquette and Louis Jolliet, sailed down the Mississippi River in their canoes. Five years later another Frenchman, La Salle, built a fort near Peoria Lake. The French ceded the land to the British in 1763. Illinois became a state in 1818.

Abraham Lincoln came from Illinois, as we all know. He returned home from the Black Hawk War and went into politics soon afterwards, encouraging the development of his state to such a degree that he later became the President of the United States. His life story is too well known to repeat here.

Let us then turn again to Chicago, called the Windy City because it is situated on Lake Michigan. It serves now, through lakes and canals, as a pathway to the Atlantic Ocean. It is in that sense a port, the world's largest inland port; at the same time it is a national center for railroad, air and truck transportation. Beyond that, it is a primary center of industry for numerous products, too many to enumerate here, but they are made and transported from some fourteen thousand, five hundred factories.

Chicago is also an educational center with its fifty-eight colleges and universities and eight hundred technical schools. It has in fact every sort of institution, including some twenty-seven churches —not excessive, perhaps, for such a huge metropolis, sinful or not as the case may be—and four hundred and eighty-six parks. These parks fringe the lake and the city seems to face the scenery but its commercial center has been the Loop, a network of roads, highways and communications within which are located many businesses. The Loop is, in fact, the city's financial center.

The name Chicago comes, I am told, from an Indian word, *Checagou,* meaning strong or powerful—a very suitable idea, except there is some suggestion also that the name may have come from the strong scent emanating from the wild garlic which used to grow along the river banks. Whatever the source of its name, Chicago has survived and has maintained its incredibly rapid growth, in spite of fires, scandals, corruption and gang warfare. One feels an indomitable spirit there, an instinct for life. If a city can have charisma, Chicago has it.

Illinois is a young state, but it has passed its adolescence. It has arrived at adulthood, yet it is far from old. Landscape, village, town and city are shaped and styled. There is something to see and do wherever one goes. I think of Evanston as an example, near Chicago, with a character and life of its own. It is on the shores of Lake Michigan, near the lake port of Grosse Point. This city looks like a New England town with its lovely, quiet streets and its university, Northwestern, which opened in 1851. Or take Springfield, the capital, where Abraham Lincoln lived for twenty-five years, a typical American city as it has been called. It sits in the center of the state, and all around it

100

are productive mines and fine farmland. It is a city of graceful design in spite of its industries.

Geographically, Illinois is divided into northern and southern areas, the north a land of industries, yes, but also a land of lakes, dunes and farms that raise hogs and corn. Southern Illinois is hilly, with round beautiful slopes that make scenes at every turn of the road. There are also endless stretches of prairie, and the soil, when it is turned for crops, is black, heavy and shining as though it were oily. Perhaps its quality and appearance are the result of veins of soft coal and oil deposits. At any rate, it is fertile and it, too, supports hogs, corn and grain. Great storage vats, rising like steel castles, reveal the richness of the state's argicultural resources.

Illinois has somehow the air of peace, plenty and self-satisfaction. Why not—why not, indeed?

INDIANA

Indiana! A lovely name, musical and lingering upon the tongue. It is a beautiful State, in many ways the most typical of our entire country, or so I feel, when I am traveling through it. My first acquaintance with it had been through Theodore Dreiser, that huge complex figure, whose books I believe to be among the most enduring of United States literature. We were friends through correspondence for a while, but after I was given the Nobel Prize, this to my own astonishment, he never wrote me again. My involuntary exclamation when the news of the award came to me had been that he, not I, should have had it. I was still young and he was not. Somehow his character, so

simple, so profound, reminds me of the rich terrain which gave him birth.

Welsh, English, Scotch-Irish and German—these provided the stock which built Indiana into a prosperous community, hearty and tenacious. It

is called the Hoosier State, for reasons into which I inquired for some years, and to my question I have received different answers. The most plausible reply, I concluded, is that the name came from one Samuel Hoosier, a contractor, who worked on the Ohio Falls canals and employed as many men as possible from Indiana because they were good workers.

Whatever the origins of the name, the fact is that Indiana is, perhaps, the most American of all our states. It is typical especially of the inland states. The sea inevitably affects the lives and characters of those who live near it, but in Indiana, the contrasts in the landscape partake of all other aspects—the prairie in the west and the flats of the north. The central part of the state as well as the north are good farming country, and the farms are well kept, the farmers progressive. Great areas produce mint and onions in profusion. The northeast is picture land, gemmed with small clear lakes and studded with mild little hills. My own favorite area—for beauty, that is—is the region toward the south, where stand closely together the spectacularly beautiful, irregularly shaped hills that painters love to portray on their canvas. I have heard of but unfortunately have never seen for myself the "singing sands" of the northwest, near the grain mining area of Calumet. I am told that the shifting dunes are a sight that should be seen and perhaps, some day, my wandering spirit will lead me there.

As usual, however, my deepest interest is in the people. Each state shapes its own people by its history and landscape, but inland people have a certain insularity, I believe. Surrounded by land, they have the immensity of the sky above them but few of them may ever soar into its distances. The sea, however, offers possibilities of a beyond and people who live in a coastal state have dreams that inland people do not have, or cannot. Indiana was once under the sea, we know. The rock base under its land is sedimentary. One must dig deep to find this base, for thousands of years have passed since it was formed. It is glacier country, too, and scientists tell us that long ago, in the Pleistocene Age, most of Indiana, except that portion south of its center, lay under a burden of ice that was one thousand to two thousand feet deep. But glacial land makes good farmland, the weight and motion of glaciers pulverizing the soil to fine, deep topsoil. Upon such land grow many kinds of trees and flowers, and these nourish in turn many kinds of birds. I was interested one June to see growing in Indiana a Chinese tree, known as the rain tree, which blooms in early summer with golden blossoms upon its drooping boughs. Upon inquiry I found that indeed this tree had been brought from China by a William Maclure, who planted it at New Harmony, the site of early experiments in communal living. At any rate, this part of Indiana is somewhat like the rich inland area of China where was my childhood home.

Of course with all this, Indiana is a rich state. It has plenty of water, good land in farm and forest, steel mills, coal and natural gas, many fine quarries of limestone for building or making lime, cement and clay—Indiana has them all. Its limestone has been used in the United Nations building in New York City. And the people thrive as a result. Resourceful, with manifold talents and capacities, they make fine Americans. I was impressed by their optimism, perhaps the consequence of living in a richly endowed environment where, if one resource fails, there is always another. Naturally, such wealth tends sometimes to develop a tinge of self-satisfaction. But that is an American quality, perhaps? At least, so I have heard abroad!

IOWA

Iowa is a beautiful State. I have traveled it in summer and winter and found its seasons reliable. I think of it too somehow as a typical American state, if any state can be typical in our varied nation. The climate is cool, even in May, but the nights can be very hot in midsummer. Snow falls heavily in winter, but the main roads are kept open.

In size, it is about one-fifth larger than the state of New York and one-fifth the size of Texas. Its agriculture is abundant and its rivers keep the land well watered. The rivers flow eastward toward the Mississippi and westward toward the Missouri. The Des Moines River reminds me of the Missouri, in summer a shifting sea of mud and in spring a rushing torrent, sweeping away every low branch and uprooted tree, and dragging away rich farmland except in areas in the northeast and southwest. It is a state blessed with ample rain, making the land fertile.

Iowa is rich, too, in its wildlife. There are few large animals but fish are plentiful, I am told, and so are a variety of birds, both shore and inland. The lakes in the northwest are especially beautiful for they serve as gathering and resting places for migratory birds. I am more interested in flowers than in animal or even bird life, and Iowa has always delighted me with the abundance and variety of its flowers. Each season brings its own blossoming specialities, and these change too, with their locale. The northern states contribute their flowering seeds to the northern regions of Iowa, and in its southern areas, the southern winds have carried seeds from the southern states. Watered plain and grassy prairie have their floral shows: the wild rose is Iowa's state flower.

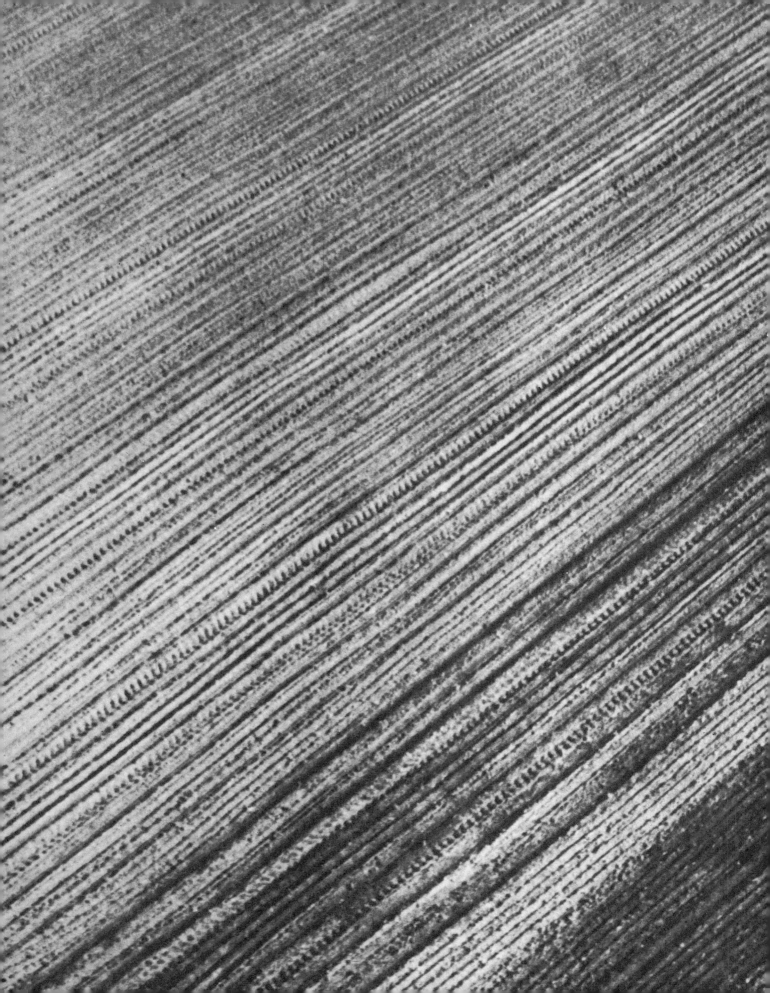

Like so much of our country, Iowa was once under primordial seas. The fact that the rock formations in different parts of this state slope in different directions, as well as the variations in the rock, leads one to believe that different seas at different times covered the land. It is of course glacial country.

The soul and the meaning of any state, however, is to be found in its people. Richly rural as Iowa is, with spacious farms, big barns and comfortable white farmhouses, modern times have brought an increased industrialization. Perhaps this is partly because Iowans have always been interested in educational and cultural activities. The land was thrown open to settlers in 1845, many of whom were from New England, that source of intellectual and cultural policies, and their first interest, once their livelihood was established, was in education. Many small colleges were established, and today the University of Iowa is among our best universities. The work done there in the area of the theater has been notable, as is also the music and art.

Iowa is remarkable, too, in its humanism and tolerance. Later immigrants came from other states and from many countries in Europe, each group bringing its own culture to enrich the whole. None met prejudice, and the effect of this favorable atmosphere is that young Iowans tend to remain within the state instead of leaving it for other areas. The result, too, of all this is an air of

prosperity, contentment and optimism in Iowa, which the traveler can share as he proceeds over its fine highways. At least I always feel that atmosphere of serenity and maturity in this beautiful state. The people are courteous and intelligent. There is no childish boasting such as I find sometimes in younger western states. The Iowans know themselves and what they are doing. They are doing well.

It is said that the great Sarah Bernhardt was born in the small town of Rochester, near Iowa City. Her mother, it is also said, is buried in the cemetery there. Legend has it that the famous daughter came sometimes to place flowers on the grave of Mary King, her mother. Whether this is true I do not know, but it is true that Sarah Bernhardt performed, one golden day, in Iowa City.

My own interest in Iowa centers about the extraordinary number of writers who were born in Iowa or who established their homes there later. Hamlin Garland wrote his stories there and

Paul Engle his poems. In addition, I can cite Susan Glaspell, Alice French, Ruth Suckow, Carl Van Vechten—the list is too long to enumerate. Suffice it to say that the rich earth of Iowa, the strong and fertile landscape, the permissive atmosphere free of the binding effects of religious or racial prejudice, the deep cultural love of the arts developed there through the influence of many European immigrants, have fostered the natural instinct of those who were born to create.

Without ostentation and fanfare, and by good organization and solid achievement, Iowa is one of our greatest and most representative states.

KANSAS

Kansas is a State very special to me, and my experiences there continued through many years. They began with the fact that my husband was born there. Since I was reared in China, I have always believed, as the Chinese do, that the place of one's birth has a lifelong influence upon one's personality. Therefore, the better to understand my American husband, I wanted to get to know Kansas. To indulge me, he agreed that we would spend some weeks each year in the state, and this we did for a number of years until I came to feel almost at home there. We traveled in our car, wandering where we liked, stopping at country inns or in city hotels. I saw that Kansas is a plateau, sloping up toward the Rocky Mountains. The western half is quite different from the eastern. Westward lie the prairies; the soil is sandy and the climate is dry, as it is in most of the Great Plains of which this state is a part. It is a great wheat growing area, and because of this is known as the Breadbasket of America. The eastern half of the state is hilly, lush and green, with black soil and many lakes.

The people of Kansas are quite distinct in their characteristics. Indeed, I have found this true for people in each of our states, and I pride myself on being able to guess, without being told, which state a person comes from. In Kansas, I found the people honest, direct, hard-working, plain in speech and simple in ways of life. Again and again I was surprised on being invited into a small plain house to find there people of education, and working perhaps in important positions. Of recent years, of course, the United States Tactical Air Command has established its bases here. This is a far cry from the first explorer into Kansas, a Spaniard named Francisco Vasquez de Coronado, who came in 1541 looking for gold.

115

The outcome of all my travels in this handsome and industrious state was, of course, a novel. For me it was a very special novel, growing slowly in my mind over a year. It was the first of my novels about my own country and I wrote it under a pseudonym, John Sedges, in order to escape the stereotype into which literary critics and the reading public were beginning to shape me. I poured all my knowldege of Kansas and its people into *The Townsman*. The story centered about the town of Lawrence which has had an interesting history of its own. It was first meant to be the state capital, and was named after one of its most respected citizens, after having been established by the New England Emigrant Aid Company. It had a stormy life until after the Civil War, but since then, it has been the peaceful center for the University of Kansas and the educational influences, and for trade and history.

My book, *The Townsman,* is a long, historical novel about a westerner who is neither a cowboy nor a gangster. I do not believe Kansas was settled only by gangsters, rowdy cowboys, drunkards and other punch-happy characters. So solid a state was built by a solid, hard-working, honest people. Not all of the true West was "wild" or built by wild men. My proud moment came when, after the publication of my book, it received fine reviews of which the finest, to me, appeared in *The Kansas City Star*. It said that "only a writer who had lived a lifetime in Kansas could have written this book."

Abilene was a place famous in its time as a cowboy town. There droves of cattle arrived on foot to be entrained for eastern markets. It was, of course, the sort of town that is dear to television westerns today. But such rough life has ceased even in Abilene. Wild Bill Hickok helped to end it by establishing law and order in the 1870s. Now the city is chiefly famous for being the childhood home of President Dwight D. Eisenhower.

Dodge City is another town with a rip-roaring

past. The city, named for Fort Dodge, was in bison area. More than twenty-five million of these animals, I am told, once wandered the plains. They were slaughtered for their hides to such an extent that, by 1875, they were almost extinct. Dodge City was known as the Cowboy Capital of the West; so many deaths took place there as a result of the cowboy quarrels, depicted on today's modern television, that Boot Hill Cemetery was established for the burial of those killed. Today the town is the staid center of the wheat-growing and cattle markets.

I remember Emporia because of William Allen White, who was a friend of mine and whom I visited briefly when I passed through this city. His house is a pleasant one of a Victorian Gothic architecture in Colorado sandstone, and it is well worth seeing. William Allen White was, of course, the famous editor of the equally famous newspaper, *The Emporia Gazette*. The city itself is the center of a rich farming and dairy area. The Kansas State Teachers' College is also situated here.

Kansas City shares a border with a separate city that bears the same name in the neighboring state of Missouri, a very odd arrangement, in my opinion, and confusing enough so that when I am in one city, invariably, I believe that it is the other. Perhaps this is one place where a wall would be convenient? At any rate, it is the second largest city in Kansas. It is an industrial center, a grain-storage center, and has industrial areas, all contained in different industrial districts, the most notable of which is the well-planned Fairfax district.

Kansas, in sum, is one of our finest states and lives a sane, peaceful and prosperous life.

KENTUCKY

Kentucky—that State is caught in my childhood memories of life in China. I am a very small girl sitting at my mother's feet as she sews. We are on the veranda of our home on a hill outside an an-

cient city. I have just asked her what happened when she had finished high school. I have been listening avidly to the story of her life in that far-away country, America, where I was born. She pauses in her sewing.

"Afterwards?" she says, her eyes dreaming in girlhood memory. "I was sent to the beautiful state of Kentucky to a finishing school there, Bellewood Seminary for Young Ladies."

Kentucky? I have a thousand new questions—where is it, how does it look, what people live there? I know most of the answers for myself now, for I have been there more than once or twice. I have been to the wonderful caves of Kentucky, the Mammoth Cave I did not have the courage to penetrate. I was already in a bus, ready to go down under when the guide's voice informed us that we must be sure, if we entered the caves, we could keep on to the end. I listened to his account of long flights of steps, narrow passages, wondrous beauty, nine miles. . . . Nine miles? I rose hastily and left the bus, and have explored for myself since, over visits of intervening years, Kentucky's beautiful surfaces.

"Blue grass?" I remember asking my mother. "Is it really blue?"

"When it's blooming it looks blue," she said.

And so it does, blue enough to give it the name, at any rate.

Except for Louisville, the state has no really large cities. People live in enchanting towns; they enjoy life and the Kentucky Derby races. Politics, too, are a diversion and political campaigns pro-

vide occasions for gatherings and festivities. On the whole, conservatism and individualism provide the atmosphere. Public institutions are not always welcome. Even public schools were late in acceptance. A family looks after its own. These people concentrate, perhaps, on their families. At least they love to discover and trace their lineage in genealogies, and the word nepotism is unknown because it is universally practiced. Of course one gives the first chance at a job to a kinsman. This seemed natural to me, for so it was for thousands of years in ancient, family-centered China.

Where is Kentucky? My research tells me that it lies on the slope of the Allegheny Mountains, a medium-sized state, neighboring Virginia and West Virginia. It has mountains, lakes and rivers—about three thousand miles of river are navigable. The climate is temperate and pleasant, with good rainfall, rich animal and plant life, the flora even semi-tropical in the Mississippi bottoms. The hardwood forests were valuable until the beginning of the century. Since then their output has been moderate. There are extensive coal fields in both the east and west of the state, and agriculture is rich.

The history of Kentucky is in some ways unusual, especially as it concerns the mound-building Indians as revealed in pre-historic excavations and artifacts. It was the first state to achieve statehood west of the Appalachian Mountains. The story of frontiersman Daniel Boone is popularly known, as is Aaron Burr's, who, after he had killed Alexander Hamilton in a duel, came to Kentucky to plan, or plot, an independent empire in the Southwest, for which he was arrested and brought to trial. Slavery in its time was always a political issue and, after the Civil War, carpetbaggers became a menace to the restoration of peace.

In agriculture Kentucky was long a one-crop state, that crop tobacco, but farming became diversified as time went on, although not without some struggle. The population is still largely rural. Kentuckians, it appears, prefer the pleasures of open space and independence. Manufacturing and mining provide opportunities for the less rural-minded. And, of course, there is always the breeding of thoroughbred horses. The first of these came from mideast Asia and were celebrated for their speed and lightness, in contrast to the thickset Norman horses of England, which were bred initially for knights in heavy armor. Arabian horses thus were preferred for Kentucky stock and have proved to be one of the money-making treasures of the state. The Bluegrass horse farms, what beautiful farms they are with their white fences, green paddocks, great trees, handsome houses and big barns.

The arts—artists, writers, songwriters and their creations—have long flourished and still do in the climate and welcoming environment of Kentucky, and architecture is particularly fine both in public and private buildings. These are in striking contrast to the simple cabin in which the great President, Abraham Lincoln, was born. This cabin, by the way, is part of a memorial in the Abraham Lincoln Birthplace National Historic Site, and it was dedicated by President Theodore Roosevelt on February 12, 1909. The completed memorial was dedicated by President William Howard Taft on November 9, 1911.

There are many interesting historical tours through this storied and beautiful state, and in its own way it is a national recreation center—Kentucky!

LOUISIANA

Louisiana is a unique State. The atmosphere is of another world, a world familiar to me and yet enchantingly strange. It has the air of old France, and to France I am tied by love and ancestry. My maternal great-grandmother was French. I do not know her full story but she was of Huguenot blood; in a time of stress the family had taken refuge in Holland where, when she was very young, she fell in love with a Dutchman and they were married. In addition to Chinese and English my language is French.

My first experience with Louisiana was in New Orleans and, incredible as it now seems to

me, it was with a troupe of young Chinese actors. The play they were presenting was a dramatization of my small first novel, *East Wind: West Wind*. The project was a part of my own effort to bring my two countries, China and the United States, closer in mutual understanding and appreciation. I was working through an organization of my own, entitled *The East and West Association*, which I carried on until communism took over in China, at which time I closed the organization.

In New Orleans, then, we opened our play. I do not know at this distance why I chose that city, but I am happy that we did. The young Chinese actors put on a nice performance which, while not wildly successful, was pleasant and was later repeated for Mrs. Roosevelt at the White House. What I remember, however, is not so much the play as the lovely city of New Orleans. I wandered through the streets of the old French Quarter, I dined with friends at Antoine's where special dishes were prepared for me, I ate tiny shrimp such as I had not tasted since I left China, I reveled in lovely courtyard gardens, I visited friends, I remember, who lived in one of the classically beautiful old houses on the river road toward Baton Rouge—in short, I fell in love with Louisiana generally and with New Orleans in particular.

The bayou region of Louisiana is entrancing mystery. It is a network of waterways that leads into swamps where great trees lift their moss-draped arms. Birds of many varieties, their names unknown to me, live there, and I was told to beware of snakes. Avery Island has flocks of egrets which I saw for the first time on that visit. There, too, I saw Chinese banana trees and great clumps of bamboo like those I had played under as a child in China. It is a tropical wonderland.

Louisiana itself was formed by the downflow of several rivers, but mainly by the Mississippi. The state was discovered by Spaniards and later named by the French for King Louis XIV. Both peoples settled there, forming an amalgamation known today as Creoles. French settlers from Canada were moved into the territory in 1755 and they were called Cajuns. This mixture of peoples was later joined by Americans of English and German origin. But the French atmosphere prevails, modified of course by the languid heat of the climate. In some ways this languid peace, the lush foliage, the swamps, the mockingbirds, the narrow rivers, the fishing and hunting, the slow sweet calm of the people make me think of Indochina in the days when the French ruled that old country, so long tributary to China. Louisiana, too, belonged to France for many years, although Louis XV ceded it to Charles III of Spain to keep the English from gaining control. Napoleon regained it secretly in 1801, and the people of Louisiana did not know of this until twenty days before the Louisiana Purchase in 1803, when it became part of the United States. After many years of changing hands it became a state on the last day of April in 1812.

There are many interesting cities in Louisiana, New Orleans being the first, but closely followed by Baton Rouge, the capital, founded in 1707. It was named by the French in the early days because a red post there was a landmark boundary between two Indian tribes. The city today is a prosperous riverport for the shipping of the sulphur, oil and salt exports which keep the state prosperous commercially. There is a very beautiful Plantation Tour which I took once when I was visiting Louisiana, and it includes visits to fine old homes, plantations and interesting small towns. I remember especially Oakley, founded in 1799, because it was the home of John James Audubon. Here he lived, taught and painted some of his *Birds of America*. A memorial park for wildlife here has been named for him.

I began with New Orleans, however, and I must end with that magical city. It was named for the Duke of Orleans, the Regent of France, and was then the capital of Louisiana Territory. The British attacked it during the War of 1812, but General Andrew Jackson defeated them during the decisive Battle of New Orleans at Chalmette Plantation, which is now a national park. During the Civil War, the Union forces occupied New Orleans for a time.

Today the city stands, prosperous and beautiful, a treasure house of history and legend. Of course I have witnessed the famous Mardi Gras, but what interests me more is the architecture of the old houses. I remember especially Madame John's Legacy, one of the oldest buildings in the entire area, built about 1727 and restored in 1788. And memorable also is Adelina Patti's House and Courtyard, which were her home. E. H. Sothern lived in New Orleans, too. I must mention the famous Beauregard Square where on Sunday afternoons years ago slaves were allowed to meet and sing and dance and perform voodoo rites.

But space fails me to tell all the sights and pleasures of this enchanting place. Let me say only that Louisiana is a favorite state.

MAINE

Each year, if possible, I go to Maine with friends.
We have a single-minded purpose. It is to eat fresh
Maine lobster. Of course lobster is on every menu
in every inn, but we take our lobster in other
places. After long experimentation and explora-
tion, we found that the proper place to eat lobster
is not where there is a menu crowded with non-
essentials. No, the proper place is in a lobster
shack as close to the sea as possible. There is no
menu card because there is nothing else to eat except boiled lobster with melted butter. The shack
is a shack and no more. Walls and roof are of unpainted boards. The floor is the same, or maybe
is only hard sand. Unpainted wooden tables and

benches are the furniture. We walk in and sit down. The shack-keeper says nothing. He knows why we are there. He goes to the tank of boiling water and drops into it the number of lobsters we want. We wait. In a short time, the lobsters are deposited before us on the bare table. We crack the shells and eat, savoring every shred of the delicious and tender meat. For a full week we eat lobster three times a day. Then we go home and occupy ourselves for another year.

What else is there in the State of Maine? The most beautiful coastline in the world, I believe. The sea has bitten deeply into Maine land, cutting lovely coves where the water is cold and clear. The rock of the cliffs holds firm, the sea attacks in fierce waves and dashing spray.

Maine is not just the land. It is also the sea. There is an eternal struggle between the two. Neither quite wins, neither quite loses. The result is not only the jagged coastline with its lovely coves and cliffs. There are also the islands. Maine is fringed with islands. They band about her like a necklace of gems, islands so beautiful with trees, rocks and small sheltered beaches that anyone who sees them longs to become an islander. Many yield to the desire and buy an island. They seldom live there year round because most people like their conveniences, which islands rarely provide. But knowing that one owns an island is comforting; one can always go there.

There are other things to love in Maine. There are beautiful old houses, for example. I do not plan to live in Maine, for I have homes elsewhere. Yet I never see a lovely old house in Maine without wondering why I do not live in it. I think of one after the other, all built more than a century ago, made beautifully strong and handsomely de-

signed. Some of them have cupolas on their roofs, called captain's walks, from which a waiting seaman's wife used to scan the seas in search of her husband's homecoming ship. One would think these houses would be built of Maine granite, but usually they are of wood, although buildings of Maine granite are everywhere throughout other states. Granite! Somehow the sound of that word suits Maine people. They are strong and weatherbeaten. There is a hard, even sharp, edge to their tongues.

Of course, where there is so long and intricate a coastline there are seagulls. They nest everywhere, laying their eggs everywhere, but only three eggs to a nest. I do not know about the technique of this secret birth control, but I have read that it is absolute. People sometimes rob the nests in spite of this, and cook and boil the eggs. I have

never eaten a gull's egg, raw or cooked. I have read that it tastes of fish and I believe it, for I often used to eat hardboiled duck eggs in China which would have been fishy if they had not been boiled in strongly salted water and thus purified. But they were still too rich; therefore they were only eaten on a certain feast day once a year, with glutinous rice packed into a triangular shape of reed leaves. The rice had its own taste which modified the duck egg flavor.

Gulls are certainly not the only birds in Maine but they somehow symbolize this beautiful state. Gulls in flight, a lovely up-soaring cloud of white alive against blue sky, blue sea; gulls alighting on dark rocks and weather-beaten buildings; gulls following a farmer as he ploughs a field—there is an affinity here between land and sea, and it is Maine itself.

MARYLAND

Maryland is another State that reminds me of England. The landscapes are English in their rounded green hills, lush green valleys, and white-fenced pastures where horses graze in contentment. The state was in fact founded by English colonists and the atmosphere has lingered.

My experiences in Maryland have been personal. Long ago, when I was still a child living with my parents in China, I knew Maryland as the place where my charming and brilliant brother, whom I adored, had his first job. This was after he had received his master's degree from Washington and Lee University in Virginia, following in the footsteps of my father and my six uncles a generation before. My brother was principal of the local high school in the town of Onancock. Years later, long after he had gone on to a distinguished career in other fields, in his memory I visited Onancock. It is a typical small Maryland fishing village on the Eastern Shore, charming in its age and simplicity. There are many people to whom the Eastern Shore, with its superb seafood, means Maryland.

For years during a certain era in my life, I traveled regularly across Maryland to and from Howard University in Washington, D. C., where I was a member of the institution's Board of Trustees. I always knew when I had entered Maryland. The landscape immediately turned beautiful. Since my sister and her family lived in the state, not far from Washington, I stayed with her on these trips and breathed the air of Maryland, relaxing benignly. Those were the days before the Baltimore Tunnel had been built, and my way led through the winding streets of the city of Baltimore. Rows of houses, whose marble front steps were always shining white, for it seemed that women were continually cleaning them, linger in my memory. Baltimore is a charming city, expressive in its ways of Maryland life and culture.

And Annapolis—who can forget that lovely town? Once, invited to visit it by the governor of Maryland, I stayed in a historic old house and thought of celebrated people who had been there before me, poets, statesmen and famous beauties. The inns are worth visiting, too. It was at a dinner given in my honor that I tasted my first terrapin and I was a bit put off by the tiny bones which somehow reminded me of small puppies. And apropos of nothing except that the legend was told me at the dinner in Annapolis, I learned that the ghost of Abraham Lincoln follows the ghost of his assassin, John Wilkes Booth, in various places in Maryland, especially at Lauck's School in Baltimore County, where Booth had been a pupil.

Remembering, I recall that the charm of Maryland worked on me so strongly that I felt impelled once to buy a house there, an ancient white house more than a century old. A huge old tree grew by the vast front porch, and a few feet beyond it the tidal waters of an inlet to the Chesapeake Bay washed the reedy shore. It was a fine place to catch crabs and fish, and it seemed familiar to me because my brother had kept his yacht on the bay long after he had his offices in Wall Street.

Yes, I am familiar with Maryland and to me it is a gem of a state, perhaps because I love its English roots and ways, and its English traditions. It was founded by men of distinction, and such men have continued in its influence. But men and women of every nationality have played their part in the state's history. In its time Baltimore was second only to New York as an entry port for immigrants from the Old World. The state was Southern in its great plantations, tended by slaves. It was Northern in its trade and industry. English though it was, it has been affected, too, by the infiltration of Germans from the state of Pennsylvania. Yet, "When you get as far South as

Maryland," James Fenimore Cooper said in 1828, "the softest and perhaps as pure an English is spoken as is anywhere heard."

As for me, when I think of Maryland, I think also of butterflies. I have seen more butterflies there than anywhere else in the world—swallowtails, monarchs, painted ladies—these and many more abound, especially in the eastern section. But there are more productive items. Farms are abundant in their harvests and curiously enough, so are sugar maples. Beef, stock cattle and horses, especially on gentlemen's farms, enrich the agriculture.

Industry, oil and suger refineries, steel works, some coal mining, fisheries and canneries, especially perhaps of oysters, men's clothing, pianos, and many other manufactures have changed the state from a rural area into a thriving industrial complex.

What else? Several important facts occur to me, among them that religious and racial tolerance goes far deeper than is found in most states. The first school for Negro children anywhere in the country was established in Maryland in 1818. In 1867, the public schools were opened to Negroes. Goucher College for Women was founded in 1886, and several other colleges for women followed. Negro newspapers were first published in Baltimore and, by 1880, there were five such newspapers in Maryland.

These and many other liberalizing influences attest to the maturity and culture of those who were leaders in the state. The atmosphere is liberal and mellow with age, attuned to its gentle landscape and its famous history.

MASSACHUSETTS

My memories of Massachusetts are many: Summers on Martha's Vineyard and long lovely days on a sandy beach, children tumbling in and out of the gently rolling surf; Katherine Cornell, a

neighbor, stopping by with her dogs; a night in Woods Hole when World War II ended and the town went mad with joy and we were marooned because the boatmen to the Vineyard took a holiday. And Boston, a family seat, where my beloved mother-in-law expected every child and grandchild to dine with her on Thanksgiving Day. And Harvard University at Cambridge, the family college for the men of our family, my visiting my son there and taking him and some thirty of his best friends to luncheon at which everyone ate filet mignon except me. Out of this welter of memories let me elucidate a few facts!

Massachusetts—a name coined from the amalgamation of three Indian words meaning "near the great mountain." The *American Guidebook* for the state breaks this down into *adshu*, or mountain; *set*, or near; and *Massu*, or great. Everyone knows that, while Indians had been the first people living in Massachusetts, the unfor-

gettable Pilgrims were the first white settlers, although John Cabot, a Venetian navigator employed by the British in 1497 and 1498, explored Canada and gave England the "right" to North America. Others from France and Spain came and went, other Englishmen came and went; but in 1620 a small group of Puritans, finding the religious compromises of the period uncongenial, left England for America, their goal to arrive in Virginia. Instead storms drove them northward and on a gray November day the Pilgrims landed in Plymouth, disembarked, and set about building a shelter before winter began. From then on their history is a fascinating account of astute, independent bargaining with Indians, on the one hand, and with the English government on the other. Religious conviction was the driving energy, combined with shrewd business sense and a fierce independence of spirit. Isolation led them to self-government. The leader in any community was the minister and next to him were the lawyer, the doctor and the school teacher. These forces combined at the town meetings as the first governing body, and this body ruled not only on public matters but on individual behavior as well, the latter resulting in the well-known "blue laws."

Education was zealously planned and pursued. One-room local schools led eventually to universities, Harvard at Cambridge being the most famous. There was no discrimination in any school; the first brick building at Harvard was built especially to house Indian students, and one of the first graduates was an Indian. Every educational institution was solidly founded on religious principles, and while religion bound the settlers together, dissension dispersed them throughout the area. The strong spirit of independence made unanimity impossible and the force of unyielding separatism which had prompted the Pilgrims to leave England continued to drive them apart in the New World.

This mood was strengthened because of their separation from England, involuntary for a period, to be sure, for it was the troubled era of Oliver Cromwell. Only when Charles II returned to the throne in 1660 did the age of independence come to an end for the Pilgrims. It was a distressing change, for by this time they had become accustomed to self-government and had built a thriving trade and growing industries. A new colonial policy was established by England and rebellion and conflict set in in the colonies, resulting finally in their determination to free themselves entirely; thus began the successful American War of Independence.

All this explains the independent spirit of Massachusetts even to this day. The end of the American Revolution and the entry of the state to the new government then located in Phila-

delphia brought peace and prosperity. Trade with England was replaced by trade with China and with it came the building of fast clipper ships, new imports and exports, industries, new influences, ideas and knowledge of the rest of the world. These were important effects and had their civilizing forces on industry and the arts. Agriculture declined and an urban culture developed. Great writers and philosophers appeared, the Puritan oppression of the spirit gave way to the humanism of Thoreau and Emerson without abating the independence of outlook. The people of Massachusetts were overwhelmingly against slavery and the abolitionist movement swept the state.

All this changed local rule and the town meeting gave way to commission forms of government and to chartered cities. Industries created wealth and fostered learning. Women's colleges and technical institutes were added to the fine schools and colleges already existing, and free libraries in every town and city became matters of course. The list of great institutions and distinguished citizens in sciences and arts put Massachusetts in the forefront of our most sophisticated states. In many ways the state is also the most typically American in history and achievement, and in self-government.

There is so much to tell about Massachusetts—its pleasant setting between mountain and sea, its rugged rolling hills, its ports and sandy beaches, its proud Boston and busy industrial cities, the polyglot population that industries demand, the backbone of old aristocratic families, its fine architecture in beautiful old homes and buildings, its stark local factories, its rich literary life and individual literary movements led by philosophers and writers, its dissensions and contentions, its driving energy sparked always by independence and freedom of the spirit—can this be anywhere so strong, so fascinating, so enduring, as in Massachusetts?

147

MICHIGAN

Michigan is sometimes called the Wolverine State, although I do not know why since the wolverine is said to be extinct, at least in this area. The state itself, however, is very much alive in all its various aspects. It is a huge terrain, its landscapes including opposites of marshes and low plains, productive farmlands in the south and sandy slopes in the north. It was once richly forested, then stripped bare and now planted again with fruit trees. Westward is the mining country of iron and copper. Most beautiful, perhaps, is the lake country: Lake Michigan, Lake Superior, Lake Erie and Lake Huron. These give this island state many of the advantages of a seacoast, and indeed, since the opening of the St. Lawrence Seaway, it does have a direct connection to the sea itself.

The first great industry of Michigan was the cutting down of its splendid forests. Ruthless destruction of huge and ancient pine and hardwoods built fortunes for a while. When the end came, as inevitably it had to, the shorn land revealed the potential of copper. For a time, as much as half the copper in the United States came from Michigan. Then these riches too came to an end. The same fate soon faced the mining of iron, but not before thousands of immigrants from Austria, Finland, Lithuania and Wales had come to work as miners and, as the mines gave out, stayed on, jobless.

Farming was tried as a substitute but limited areas were productive. Specialized crops were developed, spearmint and peppermint, beans, grains for the developing breakfast food firms of Battle Creek, celery from Kalamazoo, and salt from the deposits in the southeast and east. But industry gave the best respite for workers. Furniture in Grand Rapids, fisheries in the Great Lakes and finally the automobile industry in the Detroit area, where great companies have concentrated their production, these have provided a changing environment for the people of Michigan. To all this must be added the tourist industry for visitors abound in this state. Indeed for a time tourism was its second most productive business, and it still is to a great extent, for hunting, fishing, sailing, camping and vacationing are very actively followed. Towns and villages are devoted to the tourist, and summer plans are based on his happiness and welfare.

If any Michigan citizen reads these last sentences, however, he or she may deny it. Or they may simply declare that tourism is a job like any other, as all they are doing is their job, that is to say, a way of making a living. But this new way of making a living enables the people of Michigan to rebuild their land, reforest their mountains and restore the purity of their matchless lakes. So be it! Meanwhile they must strive to keep their fine atmosphere, for the state's climate is controlled by the four Great Lakes, the waters of which drain the heat from the warmer air, and warm in turn the colder air. The winds from the west, for example, blow cooled over Lake Michigan in summer and warmed in the winter, thus creating a wide fruit-growing belt for this tempering prevents early frosts. In the spring the cooled waters hold back the budding of fruit until the danger of frost is over. This makes for a long growing season for almost all plants, except cotton.

The early history of Michigan's pioneers is fraught with wars with the French, British and Indians, for the French had planned to establish a vast fur-trading empire which included the area occupied now by this state. The English prevented this finally when the French in 1760 surrendered to them in Montreal. The British then took over Michigan and with it the lucrative fur trade the French trappers had built up. Indeed, the growth and expansion of settlements was forbidden so that the forests could be preserved. Michigan, aided by the Indians, was at first on the British side in the American Revolution. The struggle that ensued was closed only by the Treaty of 1783, although the Detroit area continued under their jurisdiction until 1796, when England finally withdrew from the United States territory. This land had to be won again, however, from the Indians. In 1837 Michigan was admitted to the Union.

152

In reflecting upon the history and development of this great state, I perceive that I have overlooked one of its important resources, which is salt. In the eastern and southern portions, mainly, and less widely elsewhere, there is an underlay of porous rock which has, it seems, unlimited quantities of brine in it. This, even in the early days of the Indians, was processed by evaporation into good pure salt. It is mined, and also pumped. So ample are the stores of Michigan's salt that geologists tell us the state can furnish the world with salt for thousands of years ahead. But so pervasive are these salt deposits that they have interfered with the development of oil and natural gas resources, also found in these same regions.

Today Michigan is aware of the necessity for the conservation and wise use of her extraordinary resources. She is also aware of the potentials for recreation in her more than two thousand miles of fresh water shoreline and her more than five thousand islands, a playground ample enough for a nation. To this end fine highways have been laid and pleasant inns have been built, all this in addition to a solid foundation of modern agriculture and industry.

MINNESOTA

When first I went to Minnesota, it was to meet
with business associates in Minneapolis. I went by
air. Now as much as I dislike airborne travel, for I
am an earthling, I have to travel a great deal by
jet or small plane. I have crossed the oceans, east
and west, many times. I have traveled north and
south, not only in my own nation, but in such
countries as India where local airplanes provided a
rougher air journey than when I took the short
trip from New York to Minneapolis, changing of
course in Chicago.

I asked the stewardess, "Is it always like this?"

She considered and then answered kindly,
"Not always." Then in a moment of truth she
added, "But nearly always."

At any rate, I landed eventually in Minneapolis. There, as usual, in the interstices of time
between business conferences, I learned about
Minnesota. It is a watery State. The Mississippi
begins here. The state has more than fifteen thou-

sand lakes. They are the residue of the Glacial Age. Lovers of tall tales say they were footmarks left by Paul Bunyan. Added to all this water is the St. Lawrence Seaway which ends at Duluth, making the city a busy seaport.

Minnesota's growth and wealth is based on lumber, and has ranged from hunting fur-bearing animals to farming and, finally, to mining and manufacturing. During this growth, the area

went through Spanish, French and British settlements and control until, in 1849, it became a United States territory and finally, about ten years later, an American state. The early Indian name for this area was Land of the Sky Blue Waters. Today this romantic name endears itself to those who come here for vacationing and its concomitant joys of fishing and sailing.

On later visits to Minnesota, which I took by

car, my favorite means of travel, I learned of various sports which interested me for personal reasons. Blue Earth, for example, is a very small town, the seat of Faribault County. It has its name from a bluish-green clay which Indians dug out of the Blue River rocky gorges. Or Brainerd, for another example, a town that had been in the very center of a great hunting range once used by the Indians, and is now in the very heart of Minnesota. It is a railroad center, too, named for the wife of a railroad official, and even has a Paul Bunyan Center. It is also the center of an area of some four hundred and sixty lakes.

Duluth is of course a famous trade center. It has forty-nine miles of docks and on them fly the shipping flags of many nations. It is Minnesota's gateway to the world, and this access to other nations, their products and their ways of life, have made Minnesota one of our most modern and wealthiest states. The harbor at Duluth is protected by high cliffs and it is the shipping center for iron ore, coal, and many agricultural products, chief of which is grain. There are two entrances to the port, one directly from Lake Superior, and the other by way of a canal. The city's history began with French explorers and fur trappers, and was named for Sieur du Lhut who, among others, landed here in 1679.

Minneapolis is the largest city in the state, and within its city limits there are twenty-two lakes and lagoons. The campus of the University of Minnesota is the center for many cultural activities—concerts, ballets and lectures. I might also mention that there is an interesting American-Swedish Institute here which illuminates the history of the American-Swedish people.

St. Paul is of course the capital of the state. It is a quiet city with middle-class homes and tree-shaded streets. The home of Governor Alexander Ramsey is an excellent example of dignified domestic architecture of the 1880s.

What else? Searching my memory at random, I remember that the Oliver H. Kelley Farmstead is in the little town of Elk River. It was the birthplace of organized agriculture, through the nationally widespread Grange.

Grand Rapids is of course well known for a certain style of furniture. It is the center of logging country and also the point at which the Mississippi River becomes navigable. The Chippewa National Forest is there, a magnificent spread of pine trees interspersed, for the most part, with many lovely lakes. Sugar Hills is a pleasant all-year-round recreation place.

The town of Hibbing is the center of the state's mining industry. It has the world's largest open pit mine and this pit, I was told, produced a fourth of all the iron ore mined in the United States during World War II.

I remember Le Sueur because here is, or was, the home of the famous Dr. W. J. Mayo, on Main Street. Some visitors may be more interested in the fact that the jolly Green Giant is here, who—or which—puts up more corn and peas than any giant in the world.

Minnesota is a delightful, prosperous, vigorous state, inhabited by citizens to whom these same adjectives can be applied.

MISSISSIPPI

This State is associated with a vague memory that once a paternal uncle, one of six, was a Presbyterian minister in the town of Corinth. Since all my uncles seemed, during my Chinese childhood, more or less mythological characters, I do not know whether my memory serves me the truth. It did, however, cause me to approach Mississippi, upon my travels, with a feeling of some sort of familiarity, as though I had been there before. In fact, the soft damp heat of the Mississippi River is not unlike the climate of the lower Yangtze River, on whose banks I spent my childhood.

Considering Mississippi, therefore, I find that it has a vivid history, beginning in 1540 with the Spanish explorer, Hernando de Soto, who led his men thither in his search for gold. De Soto died and the leadership fell to the Frenchman Pierre Le Moyne, who established a settlement near Biloxi in 1699. No one ever found gold, but riches lay in the fertile black soil which the Mississippi dragged down from the North and across the state from north to south. Cotton, a greedy crop, flourished on the fertile soil and produced the prosperity which provided for great plantations, beautiful mansions, all dependent upon slave labor, of course. Technology made slaves unnecessary, but cotton is still the state's chief crop, although farming is diversifying, and oil and gas are recently developed natural resources.

I must, in gratitude, not fail to mention the shrimp, oysters and other fish which provide so many delicious dishes when I visit the state. Hunting waterfowl along the coast and other game in the great forests I take on hearsay, since I am no hunter. More interesting to me is the history of this handsome state. Andrew Jackson, for example, became a hero here as a result of his victory over the Creek Indians in a final and mighty

163

battle during the War of 1812. The capital of the state was named after him.

Half a century later, more or less, General Ulysses S. Grant led his forces into Mississippi. For two years the state had been deeply involved in the Civil War, or as it was called here, the War for Southern Independence. The state was all but wrecked, all communications destroyed and pillaging rampant. Here it was that after burning the town of Jackson, General William Tecumseh Sherman declared that "War is Hell." He had made it so.

Mississippi, although it remains primarily a rural state, has many beautiful cities, towns and quiet villages. I mention only a few. Biloxi is the oldest city in the Mississippi Valley. I remember the streets brilliant with flowers, camellias, crepe myrtle, magnolia and roses. I suppose they had not been there in the days of the Casket Girls, but I like to think that they were. Flowers would have been a suitable welcome for those young women tripping ashore, eager to find their future husbands. They were called Casket Girls, or as the French said, *casquettes,* because each carried all her belongings in a little box or casquette. The young women, eighty of them, had been sent to the fort at Ocean Springs, a little to the east of Biloxi, established by the Sieur d'Iberville. He knew his men would not stay in the isolated place without women, and so had asked a French bishop to select eighty young women to go to the New World as wives for the French soldiers.

Biloxi has been a favorite resort for well over a century. Oysters and shrimp are its chief delights, as far as gourmets are concerned. Indeed, shrimp were first canned here in 1883. Beyond this there are various interesting sights and tours. I remember especially Beauvoir, the Jefferson Davis Shrine and Memorial Gardens, where the Confederate President spent the last years of his life.

Crystal Springs is called the Tomato Center of the World, and well deserves its name. The fattest, sweetest, reddest tomatoes imaginable grow there in extraordinary abundance. I visited Corinth with nostalgic interest but refrained from asking questions about an uncle of a previous generation. I do not know why this city has a Greek name and my research has not provided an answer.

Gulfport was a planned city, and planned with the best intentions as a port and railroad terminal, or so I was told. With the instinctive perversity of human nature, however, people refused to live in the neatly rectangular town and it was some years before it was finally established. It is a pleasant resort town now with various activities connected with land and sea. For me the chief diversion is the show at Marine Life, but I am not to be relied upon since I will go anywhere to see trained whales, porpoises, seals and exotic fish in tanks.

William Randolph founded the town of Holly Springs. He was a descendant of the famous Virginian, John Randolph. The Civil War left the town shattered and in ruins after having undergone sixty-one raids. The worst one was conducted by the Confederate forces, under General Earl Van Dorn, who destroyed General Grant's supply base here and thereby delayed for a year the seizure of Vicksburg. Incidentally, I was told that there had been more lawyers in this town than any other profession, and this was because of squabbles among cotton plantation owners, who lived in handsome mansions of Georgian Colonial and Greek Revival architecture.

All in all, Mississippi is a lush, pleasant place to live, provided one enjoys the languor of a subtropical climate, flowers, kindliness and a relaxed atmosphere. Of the racial inequities and the tragic undertones of history in the time of slavery and the days since, I have spoken much and have written more elsewhere.

MISSOURI

This State is a *mélange* of peoples, occupations and resources. It would be difficult to pinpoint it, except to say that, in general, it is southern. Do I have a personal recollection of it? Yes, and a very early one. When I was nine years old, we had stopped for a brief weekend visit at the home of my Uncle Hiram and his wife, in the little town of Marshall, where he was the Presbyterian minister. There I had three experiences which I remember clearly: first, there were the stories my uncle told of the Civil War, when he had been taken prisoner by the Yankees, and how he had subsisted on a diet of bean soup so thin in substance, "that we had to dive for the beans," said my uncle solemnly, a twinkle in his bright blue eyes; second, my younger sister and I slept in what I had never seen before, a trundle bed that pulled out from under the high four-poster bed where my parents slept—an enchanting experience; and third, in Marshall I ate ice cream for the first time in my life, a delicious, homemade peach ice cream. Of such small events, I have memories of a pleasant and exciting place, the state of Missouri.

And add to them, decades later, meeting hundreds of feet underground in the vast catacombs of a missile base in a western state, a nineteen-year-old Missourian lad who was a junior executive there, with the power of life and death in his young hands, and who asked if it were true that my uncle was once in Marshall, because it was his hometown too; and add to that a visit to the town of Independence, and a walk to the big white house where President Harry S. Truman lived; and I have a warm feeling for Missouri.

The Ozark highlands region of course is wildly beautiful, but not more varied than the many people who form Missouri's population —German, French, Bohemian, Irish, Scotch, Welsh, Swiss, Italian, Czech, Negro—all these make Missouri a truly American state. The Ozarks themselves are old mountains, worn and

ragged; their valleys are deep and narrow. But Missouri has many rivers and it is in the rich countryside that the fertile farms produce their ample harvests. Here, too, artists live and paint their river scenes, and not only lovely landscapes but the fabulous caverns that rivers have carved out under the ground.

The people of Missouri eat well. Fruits and vegetables, meat and fish, every kind of pie, bread and cake, their tables are loaded with delightful dishes which cannot be refused. And recalling this, I am reminded of a fine inn in Hannibal, and the memory of Hannibal reminds me of Mark Twain for whose sake I had gone to Missouri one year. I read Mark Twain as a child in China,

against my mother's wishes, for to her mind he wrote of "vulgar people." But I delighted in the antics of American children who were strangers to me and who lived in a world I did not know. Years later, for Mark Twain's sake I read Edgar Lee Masters, Fanny Hurst, Sara Teasdale, Julia Peterkin and many others, for Missouri is rich in artists and writers. When I was in Hannibal, I had walked down the cobbled approach to the Missouri River where steamboats used to anchor; by luck at that moment, one of the last of those boats steamed by and as I watched it I imagined young Samuel Clemens crying out, "Mark Twain!" as he sounded the depth of the water.

But Missouri has many names of which to be proud—Kit Carson who ran away from a saddlery shop and crossed the Santa Fe Trail; Abraham Lincoln who visited his love, Mary Todd, in 1840; William Russell of the Pony Express; Harold Bell Wright; General John Pershing; George Washington Carver; Thomas Hart Benton; Ginger Rogers—but the list grows too long. Other famous men who worked here at one time or another were John James Audubon, Robert E. Lee, Ulysses S. Grant, T. B. Veblen, Louis D. Brandeis and many another who found opportunity in this great state.

Yet, rich in history as Missouri is, she is rich in industries, too. She is wealthy in some areas but she is also poor in other areas with contrasts of underpaid industrial workers living in slums and misery, of farmers struggling with unproductive land. She is perhaps a median state, neither the richest nor the poorest; a manifold state, with resources enough to grow and develop, provided her young people do not grow impatient and leave for other areas in which to fulfill their dreams. For, the richest resource in any state is the young people. If they leave, she has no hope of growth and development; if they stay, no dream is impossible to fulfill, for the young are both the dreamers and also the doers.

MONTANA

Montana signifies mountains, but in spite of its name it is only about one-third mountainous. The other two-thirds are rolling farmland and grassy plains where cattle and sheep are raised. It is the fourth largest State in the Union, and a natural division of its landscape is created by the Continental Divide which wanders from north to south, the Rocky Mountains forming it in the north with the highest peaks on the western side. The state as a whole is at a lower level than the other Rocky Mountain states but, in common with some of those states, it has Badlands with their strange shapes, though they are not so spectacular perhaps as those of South Dakota.

The climate is, naturally, very much affected by the Divide. The mountains protect certain areas from bitter northern winds, and winter west of the Rockies is milder than it would otherwise be, but there is more rain. The state as a whole is rather well known for unpredictable weather, however, and snows may come in sudden falls as late as June, though this is unusual. In general, autumn days are warm and nights are cool, sometimes even cold, I have found. But autumns are long, dry and pleasant and winter holds off arriving until December. Of course snow falls earlier in the mountains, so the best farming areas are in the lower altitudes, where frost is more predictable and less dangerous for the sudden freezing effect.

Montana has passed through the usual pioneer stages of fur-trading and timbering and it has in common with many other states a rich mining industry. Remarkably, however, seventy percent of these deposits are located in a limited area, southwest of Helena, in Silver Bow County. Coal deposits are plentiful and are more widespread. They are the remains of great forests in ages

past. Montana, like other states in the region, has an exciting history of past ages. There are fossils of many sea creatures of the Paleozoic Age, among them seven species of the condylarth, the oldest known primate of the past. Of special interest to me was the discovery of pieces of dinosaur eggs, which had only been found, previously, in the Gobi Desert in Mongolian Asia. Of course this has meant the presence of dinosaurs in past ages in Montana, and several skeletons of these mighty beasts have been discovered. *Triceratops,* with its three horns, one over each eye and one from the snout, has also been found. But such relics of primeval times in Montana are too numerous to mention here. The fact is that the entire southern region of the state and east of Bozeman is rich in materials of paleontology. Fossils of reptilian creatures have been found in the Yellowstone Valley, and the areas where the Rocky Mountains border on the High Northern Plains are also rewarding. It remains true, however, that coal is still the most valuable fossil in Montana, that is, in material terms.

Wild flowers and wild animals still abound, and they add their contribution to the enjoyment of both resident and traveler. Indeed, there are certain animals, as for example elk and deer, which are too plentiful for man's own good for they have all but exterminated valuable forage plants. In some respects, Montana, among all the states remains the closest to basic nature. Landscape and wildlife are unspoiled in many areas, and the tourist can find there a good sampling of our natural history. The greatest threats to this wildlife are other wild creatures, lesser in size but potentially destructive. Thus the western pine beetle destroys many of the trees in the state forests. One sort attacks in particular the stately tall Douglas fir, although the United States Forest Service constantly endeavors to use the best possible controls. Much of Montana remains in forest, and most of it is in national forests. These are

timbered according to regulations and not all are accessible. There are many species important commercially and lumber is one of the state's most valuable natural resources. Of course the Forest Service also requires the continual planting and replanting of trees. Grazing land is roughly divided into lower altitude levels for cattle and the higher levels for the more nimble-footed sheep. Grazing is allowed in certain parts of the national parks, the proceeds from which go, percentage-wise, to the county and the Federal government.

Montana, in spite of snow, rain and rivers, suffers to some degree from dryness, and this has been and is regularly being remedied by irrigation, especially in the plains area. Nevertheless, agriculture is highly profitable in the variety of its livestock industry and crops. Of course coal and, in some areas, natural gas are still foremost. It is incredible but true that fifty of Montana's fifty-six counties have coal deposits. Copper, silver, gold, manganese, iron, even the rare chromite are also among the state's riches.

What of her people? It is the old pioneer story of local Indians like the Sioux, French traders and trappers in the eighteenth century. Then the Lewis and Clark expedition entered the scene and by the early nineteenth century others had ventured into the area. It is an exciting story when told in detail, as one adventurer after another appeared until the day Montana became a state in her own right. Immigrants from Europe have formed local groups. Industry has drawn to Montana the Irish and English, Yugoslavs and Finns, Germans and Italians; and agriculture has attracted Norwegians, Danes and French Canadians. They all have kept their individual customs in some manner, chiefly in the celebration of festivals, but slowly the old ways are dying out.

It is the American story, repeated again and again in our history.

NEBRASKA

The first time I crossed Nebraska it had been by car some twenty-five years ago. I was on my way to South Dakota. The day was fading to sunset and it seemed to me that I had been traveling over endless territory of flat colorless countryside, devoid of towns or even farmhouses. The car was running low on gas and I wondered what I would do if my tank became empty, for where would I find even a telephone? Where, oh where, were the people? The sky was immense, the land a dun-colored plain and, the season being autumn, there was no life or color.

Suddenly, at a turn of the road I saw a small unpainted wooden house in front of which stood two gas tanks. I was saved! I drew up and knocked on the door which was opened by a tall, lanky man.

"Can you fill up my car?" I asked.

"Sure thing," he said amiably.

Then, though sunset was near, the sun momentarily hidden behind a bank of threatening black clouds and night approaching, I could not subdue my unconquerable curiosity concerning human beings.

"Do you live here all alone?" I asked. "Sure do," he said. "Don't you get lonely?" I asked. "Sure do," he said. "Then why do you stay?" I asked. "Where would I go?" he inquired.

This seemed final. The tank was full, I paid him, he went inside the cabin and shut the door just as the sun slipped below the black clouds and, for an instant, the landscape suddenly blazed. The door reopened at that same instant and the tall man stood gazing at the bright land with a look of ecstasy on his face.

"Where *would* I go?" he repeated softly, and shut the door again.

Where, indeed, when this was what he loved? I have crossed Nebraska many times since then,

179

never to stay long, always on my way somewhere else, but I have not forgotten that man. Nebraska was and in some ways still is part of the Great American Desert, and if a man falls in love with a desert he never falls out of love with it. Think of Lawrence of Arabia! The reason I understand very well: Man is in love with the desert because only the sky is its limit.

Nebraska was discovered by those doughty explorers, Lewis and Clark, in 1804. Pawnee Indians were the population then, a warrior people, but theirs was a remarkably peaceful history with the white people. They died out not so much as a result of wars with the settlers as from diseases the white people brought with them—cholera, smallpox and tuberculosis—against which the Indians had no immunity. I am reminded of the same problem in China where measles, for example, brought in by non-orientals, were a deadly disease for the local people. Lewis and Clark had not been the first explorers in Nebraska, however. As elsewhere in the West, Spaniards had come in earlier times, and then the French in the person of the inexhaustible missionary, Father Jacques Marquette and with him Louis Jolliet, in 1673. Spain and France argued over the territory until Napoleon sold it to the United States in 1803 as part of the famous Louisiana Purchase.

For a long time Nebraska was considered worthless land, impossible to cultivate, and all sorts of legends grew out of the desolate and desert country. Paul Bunyan tales abound, one being that he bred bees to eagles and, achieving a bee as big as an eagle, he hitched it to a plow and drew a beeline between Nebraska and Kansas!

The capital of Nebraska is Lincoln. This city, the second largest in the state, was so named because Abraham Lincoln had won the case against Omaha over establishing it as the capital. It was more than a case. It was almost a battle, for an armed band of Omaha citizens came one night to try to remove the state's documents from Lincoln

to their city, but were prevented. At the time such a quarrel was understandable perhaps for, in 1868, Lincoln had only thirty inhabitants. The town grew rapidly, however, to five hundred people the next year. Another famous citizen, years later, was William Jennings Bryan. It was from Lincoln that Bryan ran for the presidency and failed, although he had three times been congressman from Nebraska. Another distinctive fact, by the way, is that this state has a unicameral legislature, the work of Senator George W. Norris. It is an efficient nonpartisan organization, avoiding the competitive delays of the traditional two-house system.

Nebraska today is a thriving agricultural state. Indeed, it is one of our most productive states, with some emphasis also on livestock. On my last trip, I took time to view, at least at a distance, Chimney Rock, a National Historic Site commemorating the Oregon Trail. The Homestead National Monument is another spot for travelers' interest. Lincoln itself is the site of the University of Nebraska and has many places to visit, as, for example, William Jennings Bryan's home, the Lincoln Monument by David Chester French, who made the Lincoln statue in Washington, D.C., the Kennard Home and a good art gallery.

North Platte was Buffalo Bill's home, and is now an important agricultural center at the fork of the Platte River.

Omaha, the state's largest city, is named for the Indian tribe which had lived here until 1854 when it signed a treaty with the United States Government. The city was for a time during the building of the transcontinental railroad a typical Wild West town, but today it is a prosperous center, the largest in the world for livestock and meat-packing.

Nebraska is no longer the wide and empty spaces I thought it was that sunset evening when I had stopped at a weather-beaten shack to fill the gas tank in my car.

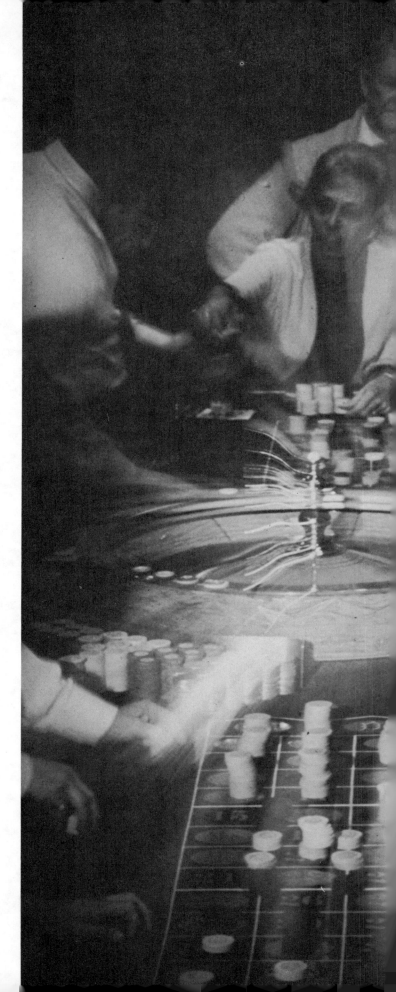

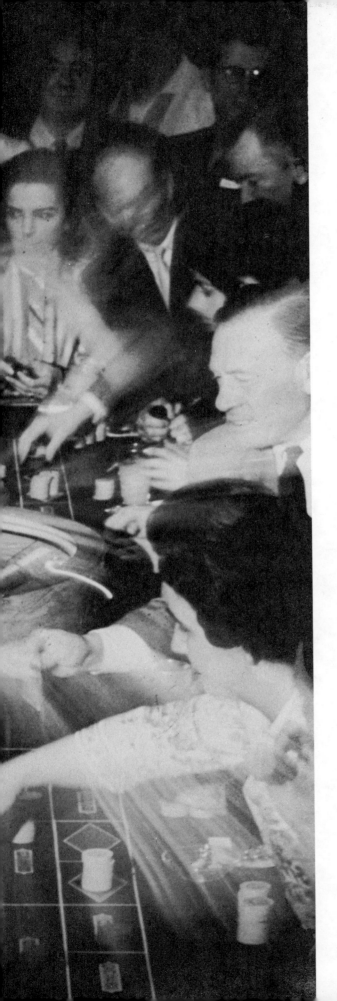

NEVADA

What do I know about Nevada? I have been there many times. I have lived there for weeks at a time. I know little about Nevada's amusement places, for they do not amuse me—I suppose because I am not amused by gambling. But I have my own knowledge of this surpassingly beautiful State. It is large in area, more than a hundred thousand square miles. It is dry and beautiful at all seasons but most beautiful in the spring when the prairies bloom with wild iris and wild peach, and the mountains are bright with blue lupine, Indian paintbrush and wild rose. The deserts are loveliest of all, for their flower is the cactus. The contrast between the stiff and sometimes thorny plant and delicate, brilliant-hued flowers is dramatic in its beauty.

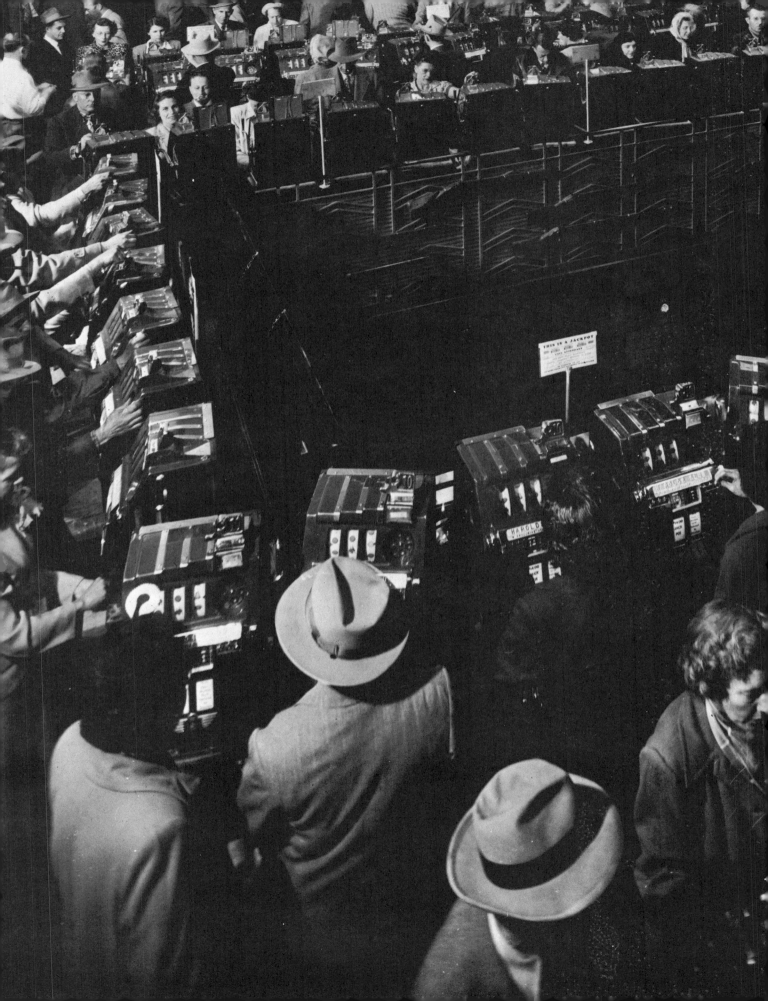

It was an astonishment to learn, among other surprising facts, that Nevada is more earthquake-prone than any other place in the world. That is to say, it was explained to me, there are more small earth-shocks here than elsewhere. People who live in Nevada, however, either do not notice them or do not talk about them. It adds to the variety of the state's many landscapes, going from lowlying deserts to mountain ranges with peaks over ten thousand feet and sometimes as high as thirteen thousand, and down again, to the deep depressions of the dry lakes, those empty bowels left, I suppose, by the receding primeval seas. But Nevada itself, the seventh largest of our states, lies within the Great Basin, a huge bowl containing a criss-cross of mountain ranges from north to south, from east to west. The rugged terrain has many famous caves which tourists enjoy, although I myself am no spelunker and can only depend on what I have heard.

My own interest in any state is primarily in its people. The landscape is important because it is the environment they either have chosen or to a degree have acquired. The people of Nevada are westerners in essence, that is, they are courageous and pioneering in spirit, although their wealth provides a surprisingly comfortable life. Many towns are really small cities where the people live in modern ease and enjoyment of the arts as well as of life's necessities. Two qualities seem to predominate in their local makeup; they are forthright, hating pretense in themselves or others, and they are born gamblers, not so much in their gambling casinos, where one can usually spot a native of Nevada by the small and prudent sums he is willing to risk, as in their inveterate and apparently incurable interest in mines and prospecting. Everyone either owns a mine or a part of one, or keeps in his house pieces of promising ore from some area where he dreams of making "a strike." A certain amount of superstition is concerned with this form of gambling, a belief in "luck," which constrained a woman who served me for a while to name one of her hopeful "strikes" after my book, *The Good Earth*. I do not know whether her faith was justified. I eventually left Nevada and she moved on to her next life.

The forethoughtfulness to which I have alluded above is exhibited, it seems to me, in at least two ways. Some forty years ago the people of Nevada had found themselves facing two problems; it was difficult for them to police the gambling areas usual in any state and they could not afford to raise local taxes. Wisely they decided to resolve the two problems with one solution for both. In 1931 they licensed all the gambling and thereby increased the state income. The gambling, I hasten to add, is under strict and enforced controls.

Similarly the people of Nevada faced the fact that not all marriages succeed in bringing happiness to the two individuals concerned. Marriage, they believe, is a private contract between two people, and when its usefulness has ended, it should be legal to dissolve the partnership honorably and legally. In other words, it is only sensible, they believe, to face life as it is and to provide the necessary means to do so.

In sum, Nevada is a state which well deserves the increasing interest visitors are showing in its extravagantly beautiful scenery and resort areas, and the variety of its vegetable and animal life. Of animal life I give only a side warning as people of Nevada have given it to me—beware the rattlesnake, its handsome looks, its menacing rattle, its poisonous fangs! Do not step carelessly from the desert road or climb unwarily into the mountains. Otherwise—enjoy, admire, and return again and yet again.

NEW HAMPSHIRE

What do I recall about New Hampshire? I pass
through parts of the State often these days when I
leave my home in Vermont, but what I remember
is the house of an old and dear friend where I used
often to visit. It was near the village of Madison,
a hamlet of a handful of New England houses
and a post office. The road to my friend's house

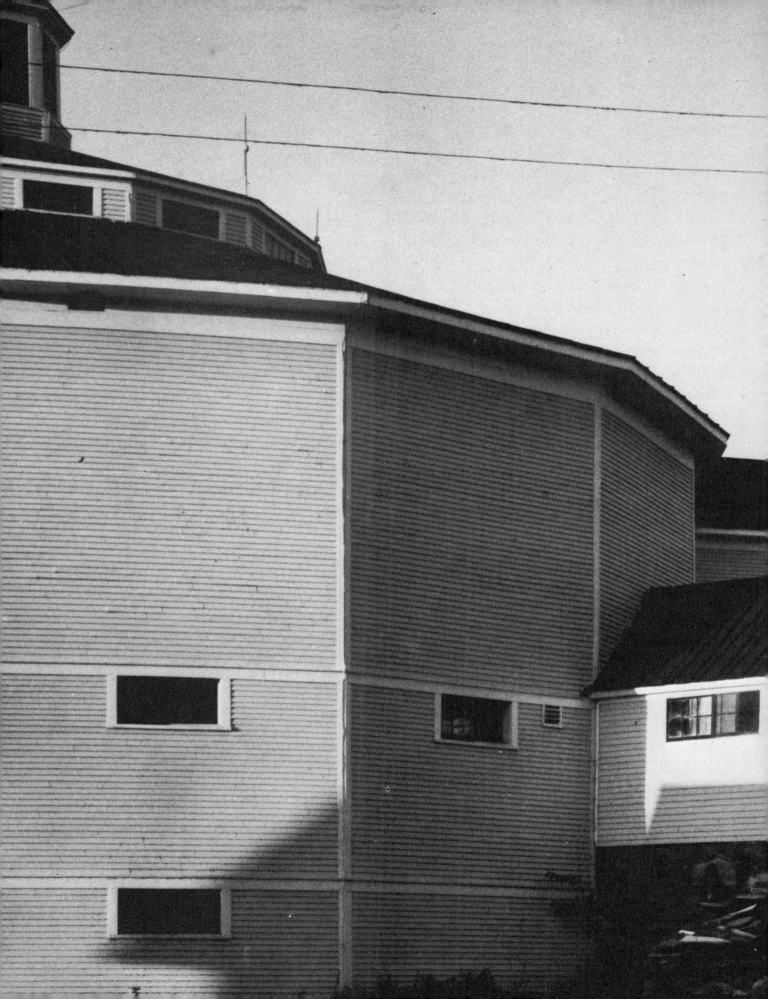

wound up the mountain and through a forest. There, to the center of six hundred acres of farmland, woods and a lake I would go, at least once a year, and before me from the terrace, the typical New Hampshire landscape would spread like a lovely, living map. On the far edge were the White Mountains, and I could see their fine lofty peaks, the highest, Mount Washington. Miles of forested hills rolled down at their feet until they came to gently sloping forests, set with gems of silvery lakes.

The lake on my friend's land was such a one, and on an autumn afternoon we would row a flat-bottomed boat over its smooth surface and, idling, we would watch the bright autumn leaves drift down and float upon the water. The chipmunks grew so tame there that they had learned to feed from my friend's hand, and cracking the peanuts with their sharp teeth, they watched us with bright eyes, wary but unafraid.

Day after day passed in this beautiful place. We traveled the state by car, stopping here and there as we pleased. My friend was an old resident of New Hampshire and he capsuled it for me as we went. It is a high state, its mean altitude a thousand feet above sea level, a mountain state, with the highest mountains in New England—not to be compared, of course, with the Rockies, but considerable. I used to visit the home of an old philosopher friend once a year or so, and from the windows of his dining room I could see the peaks of five of the highest of the White Mountains. The sunset and I had a rendezvous there and, though my friend has gone far beyond the mountains, I think of that view at that hour as a time apart, a gem in my memory.

It is also a state full of lakes, this New Hampshire. Traveling over its pleasant roads, one comes again and again upon a lake, single or enchained with other lakes. Did the primeval sea linger across the land longer here than elsewhere, I wonder, to carve out these hollows which today are

fresh water lakes? Wandering about those lakes, one after the other, I was able to learn very little about them. The people accept their state as it is, without thinking much about its history or even its future. I felt it was the least known of all the states. Even geologically too little is known. Rocky formations slant westward as though the land had been pushed up by some early giant force. Granted that I am no geologist, I always notice the giant porphyry mass, a dark grayish rock splintered into white feldspar. But its age and origin I cannot discover in any books I can find.

Among the inhabitants of New Hampshire are many animals, small and large, but my visits to my old philosopher over many years of friendship acquainted me only with his small neighbors—I should say, rather, those with whom he shared his ample acreage—foxes and rabbits, of course, and raccoons and wildcats, deer, squirrels and porcupines. He had a fondness for chipmunks, and by learning their twitter, he was able to coax them to eat from his hand, as did also robins, bluebirds and sparrows. These are everywhere the same, but he told me that on the highest peaks of the Presidential Range there are arctic fauna left by the receding ice of the final Glacial Age, and insects of the same variety as were found in the Illinoian Age. But I am no mountain climber so I cannot verify such findings.

Marble comes from Vermont and granite from New Hampshire. Both states have rich forests also, but of the two, New Hampshire is the richer if I am to trust my eyes. The great White Mountain National Forest, most of which is in this state, was purchased for $6,000,000 in 1911 by the Federal government, although, incredibly, it had been sold in 1867 for $26,000, and today is one of the most beautiful of our forested parks and national treasures. There are even some areas of primeval forests. But guidebooks have such information and I write only of what I myself know, which is all too little. Some lovely and rare old houses re-

main here and in Portsmouth, Exeter and else-where, and some beautiful churches. The first settlers were Puritans, Episcopalians, Scotch-Irish Presbyterians, and later Baptists.

The houses which most interest me, however, are the little farmhouses attached to huge barns or connected by a series of utilitarian buildings like boxes. Here in these houses, compact with all the essentials of life, families live out their generations. I am not sure whether I only imagine it, but it seems to me that the people in each state differ from those in any other. The people in New Hampshire, or so I think, are different from those in Vermont, for example. New Hampshire citizens are more gregarious and more open, less clannish and ever ready to smile, and perhaps more even-tempered than those in Vermont—generally speaking, of course. This may be the result of the rich infusion of French Canadians into New Hampshire. The French temperament overwhelms even the Puritan spirit.

When I speak of the French from Canada, I think of the polyglot town of Manchester. In truth I do not know that friendly town of many races, among them French-Canadian, Greeks and Poles, just from having visited it, though more than

casually. I am familiar with it rather because my out-of-town friends confuse it habitually with Manchester, Vermont, near which is Danby, the village where I have my New England home. How often have we in Danby accounted for a long delayed guest by remarking to one another, "Ah, he must be in Manchester, New Hampshire!" And there, in fact, he is.

Which leads me to reflect upon the lack of imagination, or perhaps rather it is homesickness, shown by the frequent use of the same name for towns in many different states. Each state, of course, considers the name of a town its singular possession, and its people may ignore the fact that there are forty-nine other states with towns often of the same name. Where the states are relatively small, as in New England, it is absolutely essential for the traveler, if he wishes to arrive at his destination, to designate the name of the state as well as the town where he is headed. We Americans are local-minded, not only nationally, but state-wise and even town-wise. I attribute this to the great size of our country and the wide variety of our ancestors. We need to be specific in order to pinpoint ourselves as individuals who belong somewhere definite in our vast terrain.

NEW JERSEY

I do not need books to tell me about New Jersey. While I have never lived there, for years my life had been caught into the manifold variety of this small, seacoast State—small in area yet with all the diversity that each of the states of the Union seems to possess. What could be more different than the crowded, industrial city of Paterson, the ethnic confusions of Newark and the wide calm beaches of Barnegat Bay and Island Beach? True, Atlantic City has its own *mélange* of beauty contests and business conventions, not to mention the amusement concessions and activities. But Atlantic City in the summer and the same city in the winter are two different places. I confess I shun its summer aspects but I have spent happy hours there in winter, walking solitary on the deserted boardwalk or sitting on a wooden bench, wrapped against the cold sea wind, to gaze at the wild winter surf.

And speaking of contrasts, shall I forget the historic beauty of Princeton? I have visited that lovely town for several reasons. A charming family there had adopted two Amerasian children in whom I was interested and who grew up there most happily among friendly people and went their ways. Aside from that, for some years it was my habit to take Sunday dinners with friends at a fine inn. But stay—years before that, when we first had gone to Pennsylvania to live, my husband used to commute to his New York office several days a week and it was my pleasure to drive him in the early morning to the railroad station and to meet him again in the late afternoon. I loved the drive beside the Delaware River and the old canal, and I always drove slowly through Princeton itself, admiring the stately buildings of Princeton University. And of late I have visited my friend, the great scientist, Dr. Vladimir Zworykin, to learn of and admire his latest work of applying to the techniques of surgery the values of electrical and electronical engineering devices.

Yes, my experiences in New Jersey have been numerous. For years we used to spend our summers on a spit of land between the Atlantic Ocean and Barnegat Bay, fishing, crabbing and swimming. It was a private island, and we lived on the bayside when the children were small. There where the water was shallow, we would tie the rowboat to the dock and the children would tumble in and out of the water, always within sight of my desk at the window. When they grew older they wanted the ocean surf, so we moved to a gray and weather-beaten coastguard house, and I would spend long happy hours on the wide beach, the dunes behind me and the sea wind blowing the tall beach grass. New Jersey is blessed in its magnificent beaches. Years later, when the children were grown and my husband dead, I bought a house in Stone Harbor, a lovely quiet town, and there for a space of years I stayed from time to time, until I no longer needed to be alone.

Today New Jersey is a fascinating complex of recreational, educational, agricultural and industrial life. It has vast shipping facilities. Oyster crackers take the name of Trenton Crackers after the city in which they are made, along with pottery and china; glass is made in Glassboro; fish of many kinds are caught along the coast; and the sandy soil of south Jersey produces the finest fruits and vegetables. Fields of blueberry bushes, raspberries and strawberries, orchards of apples and peaches, vineyards of grapes, acres of watermelon, lettuce, cabbage and spinach, potatoes and sweet potatoes—every vegetable, in short, but especially, perhaps, tomatoes, flourish on New Jersey's sandy southern soil. Generations ago an enterprising state senator, surveying the sandy earth growing nothing but scrub pines and stunted oaks, perceived that such soil resembled certain areas in Italy. More practical perhaps than most officials, he imported into the state some four hundred Italian farmers and their families. The result today is that south Jersey is one vast, flourishing truck garden, supplying rich fare to New York, Philadelphia and other cities. Of course with this lush farming goes the raising of chickens, turkeys, ducks and pigs. And being of Italian descent, many of New Jersey's farmers also make wine.

I must not forget the old houses that are to be seen along its highways. There is one near a lake and a large cranberry bog—cranberries are also a Jersey crop. I often pass this house and, when I do, I remember that it is haunted by so petulant a ghost that it is regarded as dangerous even to try to enter the door, for the intruder never gets beyond that door before he is felled. Equally strange, if not so sinister, is the area known as The Pines, where the trees never grow much higher than three or four feet; however old they may be, they stand as squat and stocky as ancient dwarfs.

Such is the state of New Jersey, a small state in all but its infinite variety of people and of place.

NEW MEXICO

New Mexico—well, I went there with a special purpose. I was preparing to write my novel, *Command the Morning*. I had made many visits to the great scientist, Arthur Compton, and he also had visited me. I had talked with Eugene Wigner, Robert Oppenheimer, Leo Szilard and others. I had gone to Oak Ridge in Tennessee. It was the talk with Oppenheimer that persuaded me to go to Los Alamos.

How well I remember that day! The heat was all but insufferable, redeemed only by the dry desert air. The sky was a deep purple blue, the bluest sky I have ever seen in any country in all my travels. Our plane landed in Alamogordo, a town encircled by the Sacramento and Oregon Mountains. We had previously landed in the capital city, Albuquerque, and I had stayed there long enough to learn something about it. It was founded in 1706 by Don Francisco Cuervo y Valdes, who was the Spanish governor of New Mexico. He colonized it by resettling some thirty families in this area where there was good pasturage. He named the place after the Duke of Alburquerque who was then Viceroy of New Spain, as Mexico was then called. Later the first letter *r* was dropped from this name. The history of the city is one of prosperity. Pasturage was good, population increased, later it became an American military outpost and later still a railroad center. Today it is a commercial center, but more interesting to me is the fact that it is where astronauts are given their qualifying tests at the Lovelace Clinic.

To return to my personal history in New Mexico—at Alamogordo, we took a bathtub-sized plane, or so it seemed to me, to fly to Los Alamos, situated on the not too distant surrounding mountains. I had never been in a three-seater before;

the pilot was in the front seat, and my companion and I were in the small two seats behind. We rose perpendicularly, the pilot talking when it seemed to me he should be concentrating silently on what he was doing, the plane bouncing up and down and right and left, a feather in the wind; we sped onward, the nonchalant pilot paying no attention apparently to his task but turning his head to talk with incessant chatter. We soared into the sky, my innards dropping earthward, and landed eventually and safely on the top of the mountain where the atomic center is perched.

"How did you find this place?" I asked Robert Oppenheimer when I reported the trip.

He said in effect that they had searched for a secluded little known spot where they could carry out in secret their scientific research for the atomic bomb, and had found for sale a boys' school in this remote spot. I stayed here for some time, absorbing its atmosphere and talking with the scientists still working there. When I left, however, it was by car and not by the bathtub plane.

Let me continue now with the history of this beautiful state of New Mexico. It had first been seen of course by Fray Marcos de Niza in 1539 in the spring, when desert flowers were in bloom. He saw from a mesa, the books tell me, a great Indian pueblo and he returned to New Spain to talk about cities of gold. The Viceroy the next year

sent an army under Francisco de Coronado to take the gold, but Coronado returned to report he could find no treasure. Various explorers subsequently came and went until 1821 when Mexico declared its independence from Spain. After the Mexican War in 1846, New Mexico was ceded to the United States and, in 1912, it became a state.

It is a handsome and in some ways a unique state, with characteristics of its own. The state is not all desert. In the south there are also green mountains. In the north, amid desert, there are mountains so high that they are snow-capped all year. Farmers and Indians speak in Spanish to each other. The remains, or rather the traces of the oldest human beings known in North America are to be found here. Indians continue to live here much as they have always lived. The Navajo Indians, however, are prosperous from uranium and oil reserves on their lands. There are several Indian tribes in the state, each trying to preserve its own way of life, but living in peace. They have among them at least six different languages.

New Mexico is a rewarding experience for the visitor. It would take years to see it altogether, so varied are its sights and cultures. At Carlsbad, of course, are the famous caverns, one of the largest cave complexes in the world and, I am told, one of the most spectacular. The caves are more than a thousand feet underground and continue for eight miles. They are inhabited by bats and probably have been for centuries.

At El Morro National Monument, there is a high cliff upon which are carved the names of early explorers as they traveled the ancient trail taken by the Conquistadores from Santa Fe to Zuni. The earliest recorded name is that of Don Juan de Onate, who carved his name here in 1605.

Sante Fe is the oldest capital in the United States; the Plaza and the Palace of the Governors were laid out and built in 1609. Nearly half of the

city's people are of Spanish descent and until 1930 New Mexico's State Legislature was bilingual. It is still a city where the atmosphere is friendly and informal in the Spanish life style. It is a delightful place and there are numerous sights to see and festivities to enjoy.

I am especially interested in Taos because many of our most distinguished writers and artists live and work in this city of three cultures—Indian, Spanish and Anglo-American. In fact, Taos is really three towns. I remember it because of the years spent here by D. H. Lawrence, one of the greatest English writers of modern times.

Taos is an old town, settled in 1615 by Spanish colonists. The houses are adobe and flat-topped, surrounding plazas, each plaza a vivid and colorful square. Among other interesting places to visit is the D. H. Lawrence Ranch and Shrine, maintained by the University of New Mexico.

But as usual space fails me to tell of all the treasures of this state, New Mexico is a glorious part of our planet, Earth.

NEW YORK

The Empire State is well-named. It is king-sized, big enough to be a nation, both in area and in population. It contains one of the largest cities in the world, both past and present, but beyond that the state has a distinguished history and the geographical advantage of its port. There was a period, however, when the rival of New York City was Philadelphia, but the foresightedness of De Witt Clinton, the nephew of New York's first governor, persuaded the men in power in the state to build the canal from the Hudson River to Lake Erie. This enabled New York to increase the flow of western trade and so established the preeminence of the state in manufacturing and commerce.

Since I grew up in bamboo groves in central China, for me one of the small but highly interesting facts about the Empire State is that on Shelter Island there grows, or grew, the only bamboo grove north of the Carolinas. This is because of the Gulf Stream current, its warmth in sharp

contrast to icy mountain slopes and snowy peaks not far away.

My years of living at least part of each year in New York City, the time I have spent traveling the magnificent parkways leading north, south, east and west, have given me a sense of familiarity with New York state and its people. Nor can I forget that once for a span of time I owned a farmhouse and acres of land in beautiful Dutchess County, and it was there I first lived for a while when I returned permanently to the United States. Hyde Park, where I visited, was not far away from the farm.

The harvests in New York are rich. Fruits and vegetables, maple sugar, chickens and ducks—including the famous Long Island duckling, are in abundance. People like to eat well in New York and some of the best gourmet restaurants in the world are to be found in New York City. Resorts such as Saratoga, founded in times past and where much of ancient glory still remains, are pleasure places for many people. Indeed, city and country combine to provide pleasure, and the variety is wide enough to suit any taste and pocketbook. Some go to Saratoga for horse racing—and some, like me, for music and ballet.

I am always impressed, too, by the number of colleges in New York state. There are more women's colleges here, I am told, than in any other state. Another interesting fact about education in this state is that instead of establishing large state universities only, New York uses privately endowed institutions to a great extent. But the entire educational system is under the regulation of the state. There are some locally sponsored community colleges.

What of the people of the Empire State? First, of course, were the Indians. Of all that I have read about Indians, I am somehow most impressed by the fact that they reveal their affinity to Asians in their love of children. The Indians, like Asians, never believed in striking a child. In these

days when the stresses and strains of modern life impel the abuse of children by adults, it is a reason to respect the Indians who considered it a crime to ill-treat children and punished the adult who committed such a crime. But we have reason, too, to be grateful to the peoples who came to New York. Every citizen of this state has reason to value and respect the sturdy Dutch, who left their mark on fine architecture and thriving business companies. The English aristocracy built handsome mansions and noble cities. When the War of Independence broke out, it was fought bravely by many Englishmen, and great museums remain

to tell the noble story to today's school children. Nor must we forget the Germans, Italians, Irish, Jews and countless others who have played their part in the building of this, our richest and most populous state.

As for New York City, it is a place apart. There is not its match in any other country in the world. And, with the United Nations, it serves as the world's headquarters. Its skyline is unique and has been copied everywhere on other continents. Its skyscrapers have been built by descendents of Indians and by newly arrived immigrants. It has set a world style in living. It is huge enough and diverse enough to provide what anyone desires to find. It is the center of business and finance for businessmen. It is one of the great seaports. For artists, writers and musicians it is a world mecca. It has concentrated wealth and yet it contains centers of desperate poverty. It has some of the most magnificent buildings and parks on earth and the filthiest streets of any city I have ever seen anywhere in the world. It has broad plazas and crowded ghettos. It is a city of such wild contrasts of religion and crime, beauty and ugliness, extravagance and destitution that it excels, too, in extremes. It is New York City, emblem and symbol of the Empire State.

BROADHURST
MAJESTIC
Fiorello!
A New Musical Comedy
THEATRE
JACKIE GLEA
WALTER EILI
PIDGEON HER
PETER GLENV
PRODUCTIO
TAKE ME ALO
LIBERTY
THEATRE
TICKETS
TAKE ME
ALONG
MUSICAL

NORTH CAROLINA

It has never been made clear to me, either by books or by people, why and how it is that the fifty states of our great Union are each so distinct in character from the other. Historically and even geographically some explanations can be made, but how explain the differences in the people, in their attitudes and opinions, in their life styles, in the very atmosphere they create, mentally and emotionally? Nowhere is this more true than in North Carolina. This State is very different indeed from Virginia to its north and South Carolina to the south, because its people are individualistic and unique. They have not the aristocratic complacency of their northern neighbor nor the careless self-satisfaction of their southern neighbor. They are progressive, industrious and ambitious. They have some of the finest universities in our country and they concern themselves with the cultural aspects of arts and crafts. Moreover, North Carolina is a scenically beautiful state, with sea and mountain to provide contrasts. The people are delightful, a reasonable, intelligent, modest citizenry who are, nevertheless, quite aware of their own achievements, their progressive spirit and ambitions.

The state has an interesting history. The first settlement was on Roanoke Island in 1585, but was later abandoned. The next attempt was made in 1587 and these settlers simply disappeared, leaving no explanation except the word *Croatoan,* crudely carved on a tree. Perhaps the Indians killed them. Later English, German, Scotch, Irish and African immigrants came in, bringing with them their various religions as Quakers, Moravians, Episcopalians and Presbyterians. Some of the descendants of these peoples still live in the mountains, singing their old songs, and practicing their old faiths. North Carolina, while a southern state, was never immersed in the business of slavery nor was her agriculture dependent on slaves. Not many North Carolinians owned slaves, few owned many, and free Negroes were accepted as part of the scene.

My first acquaintance with North Carolina was many decades ago. I was a junior in college in Virginia and had finished a strenuous year not only in my college work but also as president of my class. I wanted a vacation in some spot where I

had never been, and homeless as I was, since my parents were far away in China, I decided to go to Asheville, where friends on furlough from China tended to congregate. Thither I went and stayed for three months, exploring, learning and enjoying the magnificent scenery.

My next contact with the town was decades later when, having left China when the communists entered, I returned to my own country to live. Then I became interested in Asheville as the home of Thomas Wolfe and the scene of his most powerful novels. Asheville is also the seat of Buncombe County, which was the source of the opprobrious word, "bunkum," innocently created by a windy politician of that area who, when asked why he had made so long a speech upon one occasion without actually saying anything, replied that he "had done it for Buncombe." The Thomas Wolfe Memorial is in Asheville, and so are the Biltmore Industries Homespun Shops and the Southern Highland Handicraft Guild, all worth visiting if one is so inclined. In spite of *You Can't Go Home Again,* the town is proud of its celebrated author and the Thomas Wolfe Playhouse has been named after him.

There is, however, a great deal to see elsewhere in North Carolina. Cape Hatteras and Cape Lookout National Seashores, are rich in wild ocean scenery and there are lovely mountain drives and parks.

My own interests led me, however, to the universities and specifically to Duke University in Durham, and there to Dr. J. B. Rhine and his experiments in parapsychology. His helpful wife lives with him and together they showed me the remarkable results he has achieved, mainly in the area of mental telepathy. The university is of course named after the wealthy Duke family, its benefactor. The town of Durham thrives on the many industries owned by this family, chief of which is tobacco. The scent of cured tobacco makes the very air of the town fragrant.

Fort Raleigh on Roanoke Island is a National Historic Site, because the first colony made its home here. The first child born here of English colonists was Virginia Dare. As I have written earlier, the settlement mysteriously disappeared. Its governor had gone to England, a few days after Virginia Dare was born, to get supplies and was delayed in his return by the war between England and Spain. When he did get back in 1590, all were gone.

The Great Smoky Mountains National Park is beautiful beyond description, terrifyingly beautiful, but I drove through when the roads were as yet unfinished; perhaps now the drive is not as terrifying and only the loveliness remains. The park is in the Appalachian Mountains, eight hundred square miles of beauty, part of it in Tennessee. The mountains are more than two hundred million years old, I was told. I was last there in the flowering season, and upon hearing that there were some thirteen hundred different species of plants, I believed it: mountain laurel, rhododendron and wild azalea were ablaze. The views were stupendous. Outstanding were Newfound Gap and Clingman's Dome.

Greenboro, a sizable city, I recall is near the birthplace of the great short story writer, O. Henry, whose real name was William Sydney Porter. It is an industrial town of Quakers, Scotch-Irish and Germans. One more memorable item— it was here that Jefferson Davis, President of the Confederacy, settled the terms of the surrender to the Union in 1865.

Raleigh, of course, is the capital of the state. It is a busy commercial place but rather beautiful, nevertheless, and named, as everyone knows, for Sir Walter Raleigh. It is the administrative center of the state but also a center for educational institutions.

In sum, North Carolina is a handsome and progressive state, one of which Americans can be proud.

NORTH DAKOTA

I was on my way to Bismarck to keep a lecture engagement. We were coming by car from Oregon. The season was late autumn, in November. The start that chill gray day had been late. Another lecture the night before had been late. The inn where we had spent the night had been slow about serving breakfast. We were on our way, however, with barely enough time to make Bismarck in time for me to change and get to the lecture hall. Luncheon would have to be a quick hamburger somewhere along the way.

We started, I in good spirits for I saw no high mountain peaks on the horizon. I have a phobia about heights, the result of having been carried as a child in a bamboo sedan chair, suspended on bamboo poles resting on the shoulders of Chinese chair-bearers, looking down over seemingly bottomless chasms. The roads, winding in violent curves, had been rocky footpaths broken up by steep steps. No such horrors faced me that day in North Dakota, however. There was no snow, though the sky was clouded, and we motored along a fine highway at good speed.

All went well until, suddenly, we were on top of a mountain! We had been traveling unawares on a rising plateau, the road safeguarded by pleasant banks on either side. Now we were caught in a narrow pass, on the one side clinging to a high ascending cliff, on the other an appar-

ently bottomless gorge from which not even a barricade protected us. Moreover, the highway was fast becoming slippery with ice, snow had suddenly begun to fall and we had no snow tires.

My companion, who was driving, muttered between his closed teeth, "Shall we go on?"

I peered down into the gorge. Between clenched teeth I muttered back, "We can't turn. There is no room."

The endless crawl, it seemed endless, went on for over an hour. Fortunately we met no car coming the other way for we could not have escaped death. I arrived at Bismarck, stepped straight onto the speaker's platform, several thousand people waiting, and gave my lecture.

Afterwards I discovered Bismarck to be a pleasant city, not large but strikingly modern. Its capitol building is especially handsome, a skyscraper of excellent design. The city is in the middle of an area of large and successful farms. Its products are merchandising, beef, wheat, farm machines, oil, hydroelectric power, lignite, and so forth. It also is the administrative center for the oil industry which began in 1951.

Its history is interesting. The name was given to it in the hope, a vain one, that Bismarck of Germany himself might be flattered enough to persuade German commercial interests into building transcontinental railroads here. Aside from this, in 1804, the Lewis and Clark Expedition made an encampment in the vicinity, President Theodore Roosevelt visited and carried on his usual riding and hunting activities hereabouts—a national park bears his name in the state—and various other well-known persons, among them Chief Sitting Bull, contributed some of their fame to Bismarck. What interests me more, however, is the geographical fact that a certain span on the east bank of the Missouri River, near the center of the state, is within a hundred miles of the exact center of the Continent.

To return to North Dakota itself, the state is

mainly prairie land. Ranches are huge, cities are small, farmhouses are small, too, and wheat lands are seemingly endless. In modern times great dams have harnessed the biggest rivers, the Red River and the Missouri, creating veritable inland seas. The Oahe Dam in South Dakota, for example, has backed the waters of Lake Oahe almost to Bismarck.

The earth is North Dakota's treasure. The rich soil produces not only several varieties of wheat and other crops but crude oil and soft coal, or lignite. The history is not greatly different from that of other states. Spain, France and England made their claims and had their contentions. The French Canadians explored and trapped for furs. The area was part of the Louisiana Purchase, however, and the indefatigable Lewis and Clark established the first fort at Fort Mandan. The first settlement was Pembina, but Fort Abercrombie made it possible for a horde of settlers to come in and gradually, in peace and in combat, to take the land from the Indians.

Among the towns of North Dakota, I remark Bottineau, the site of the International Peace Garden. The garden is partly in Canada, partly in the United States. It is a superbly planned park established as a monument to peace and friendship between the two countries.

There is also the Monument to the Four Chaplains. It is dedicated to the four brave young men who were on the transport *Dorchester,* when it was torpedoed off the coast of Greenland in 1943 during World War II. The monument is of special personal interest to me because one of the young men was the son of my friend Daniel Poling. Of these four young chaplains two were Protestants, one was Catholic and one was Jewish. On the fast-sinking ship, they gave up their life jackets to four young soldiers who had none.

It is a tribute to the people of North Dakota that they have had the concern and the impulse to create these two noble monuments.

OHIO

Ohio lies on a slope westward from the mountains of its neighboring states, Pennsylvania and West Virginia. Part of its soil is glacial in origin and the glacier flattened the land into rich, broad plains, yet left its debris in rumpled hills and rough moraines. Long ago strange animals roamed here,

even elephants which normally can tolerate no icy weather. Great sloths and huge mastodons left their remains in the soil of early Ohio.

This soil is rich and produces many crops, chief of which perhaps is corn. It is limestone soil and, besides corn, it grows wheat, hay and alfalfa, or indeed almost any crop natural to the climate. Early in the modern era clay was discovered and pottery and tile began to add their products to the agricultural profits. About half of the white table-ware used in the United States comes from the State of Ohio. The industry is located around Zanesville.

Untold riches of salt deposits were discovered in the beginning of the nineteenth century, and salt is still being mined with no end apparently in sight. Natural gas and oil are also in abundance. Unfortunately, the fine original forests were carelessly destroyed in clearing the land for settlement but reforestry has been taking place now on a large scale. With reforestation, flood control goes hand-in-hand. The Ohio River is prone to cause floods, but a Federal conservation laboratory in the Muskingum River Valley checks about three-fourths of the runoff there. National forests aid in flood control too, and the quieted streams and rivers are being stocked with fish.

The first people in Ohio were the Indians known as Mound Builders for the simple reason that they buried their dead in mounds, along with their tools and utensils. These mounds were more than graves, however, for there are elaborate tunnels and pits within them, whose use is not known. By the middle of the eighteenth century, French and English explorers had come into the region. They were followed by land-hungry settlers and, by the end of less than a hundred years, the Indians had been driven off and thousands of white people were occupying their lands—this after nearly a century of struggle and war not only against the Indians but among the settlers themselves.

By the beginning of the nineteenth century, there were about a quarter of a million settlers established in Ohio. Towns had been built, schools and churches established. An Ohio man, William Henry Harrison, became President of the United States. Roads, bridges and canals brought farm produce to the markets. It was a rich and burgeoning era that lacked in nothing except culture, a fact sharply pointed out by Mrs. Frances Trollope, a visiting Englishwoman and writer, and the mother of Anthony Trollope. This narrowness exhibited itself in many religious sects, all mutually exclusive. It is interesting that Joseph Smith and the Mormons found much favor in Ohio although financial difficulties led them to move westward.

The growth of Ohio's prosperity was hastened by the development of canals, railroads, the telegraph and the manufacturing of farm ma-

227

chinery. People of many origins poured into the state; they were at first mainly those of Anglo-Saxon stock but later, as steel and rubber mills came into being, Italians, Czechs, Poles, Slavs and Hungarians crowded in, this after the Civil War, during which there was much dissension. Ohio was against slavery, however, and indeed became a sort of haven for escaping slaves.

Another Ohio resident, William McKinley of Canton was elected President of the United States in 1896. His rival was William Jennings Bryan. The state was divided by political bosses, each powerful in his own region, each so powerful that, one, Mark Hanna of Cleveland all but decided who was to be the president. In fact, he stood a chance at one time, of being himself a presidential candidate.

Meanwhile, politics aside, the state slowly was developing its cultural life. Colleges opened in each major city, and the state provided its own excellent public school system. Industry increased during World War I, there were many new millionaires created, and the arts began to develop from the various ethnic groups who were of greater variety than in any other state. Music and painting, novels and poems appeared from the burgeoning industry and agriculture. Names grew famous far beyond the geographic boundaries of the state that gave them birth or fostered their rise to fame. Nevertheless, it is interesting to contemplate the famous sculptured group of figures on the grounds of the statehouse in Columbus, entitled *These Are My Jewels*. The group is composed of the statues of three presidents, two generals of the Civil War and two United States cabinet members. There is no artist or writer represented. I do not know whether this discrimination was made by the state of Ohio or whether it was a national attitude. I suspect the latter. There have been excellent writers and artists born in Ohio who, nevertheless, left it. Music is perhaps an exception, each city has a symphony orchestra,

228

but the Cleveland Symphony Orchestra of course is notable.

It would not be fair to close these reflections without pointing out that there has been a change in modern Ohio. Dramatic arts, for example, have blossomed in schools and universities. Western Reserve University, Antioch College and Ohio Wesleyan University among others have done remarkable experimental work in the theater in cooperation with the Cleveland Playhouse. There is, moreover, a certain solidity in the state of Ohio, a firmness in its agricultural and industrial promise for the future. There is no flashiness, nothing fleeting, in Ohio's approach to life. Traveling across its fertile acres, lingering in its handsome cities and towns, one feels in the very atmosphere a combination of stability and progress.

OKLAHOMA

I have memories of Oklahoma. The earliest one goes back many years to my home in Nanking, China. I was expecting a famous guest and his wife. His name was Will Rogers. I had not heard his name in China but my publisher had told me he had praised an early book of mine, *The Good Earth*. Since Will Rogers daily wrote a comment for *The New York Times,* printed on the first page in a little box, people always read what he said, so the sales of my book had shot upward. When Will Rogers came in that day with his wife, he told me they were from the State of Oklahoma. Oklahoma? I had only heard of it in a geography book.

"You look like an American Indian," I said.

"I am pretty much American Indian," he said. "Most folks in Oklahoma are."

He sat down then and told me about Oklahoma. It had quite recently became a state. Less than a century before, it had been Indian Territory under the control of the Five Civilized Indian Tribes.* Earlier than that the territory had been surrounded by Spain in Florida, France in Louisiana and England in the Carolinas and Georgia. When the United States bought or claimed these areas, the Oklahoma Indians had already become astute diplomats, accomplished in governing themselves and in dealing with the white man. Intermarriage with the white settlers meant that when Oklahoma became a state her citizenry was already a mingling of Indian and white man's blood, and still is.

After the primary period, the Oklahoma Territory went into an era of "unassigned land." This meant it was opened to homesteaders. Immediately there was a rush of young, adventurous men into the area. This is important because it meant that to the good, bold blood of the five Indian

* Cherokee, Choctaw, Chickasaw, Creek and Seminole

tribes there was added the blood of young, strong white men. It is not surprising that although Oklahoma today is still a young state, she has advanced fast and far. From the dugouts of the early settlers there came today's pleasant homes; early trails have become fine highways, villages have grown into towns, and schools and colleges have multipled.

All this, first told to me by Will Rogers, I later confirmed by my own visits to Oklahoma. Another memory—I was at the excellent University of Oklahoma one day, twenty years ago, to give a lecture. Before the lecture, there was a reception. In the midst of the crowd, a tall handsome woman hastened to me. She was a Korean and she wore Korean dress. I recognized her at once, because she resembled a beautiful baby boy who had been given to me so that I could find a home for him. She had not been able to keep him for reasons it is not necessary to relate and I had found good parents for him.

"How is he?" she whispered in my ear.

"He is well," I told her.

Strange how the links of life are forged!

For myself I found that Oklahoma, like some of the other nearby states, tilts westward to the Rocky Mountains and its rivers flow southeast to join the Mississippi. In the northeast, part of the Ozark Plateau area reveals itself in low mountains and deep, close valleys. But in the southeastern region there are mountains of which I had never heard until I visited the national forest there. They are the Ouachita Range, and they are heavily wooded and quite breathtaking. All in all, the scenery is varied, consisting of the Arbuckle Mountains, a national recreation area in the south-central portion; a piece of rough country, rocky and wild, known as the Cross Timbers; as well as prairies in the east and grassy plains in the west. The Cimarron River is especially beautiful. During World War I there was a time when much of the plains were ploughed and planted to

230

wheat. Later the area became part of the Dust Bowl. Now it is going back to its original state.

Oklahoma itself is fascinating and it should be further explored. Mankind has had a long history and we are only now beginning to know its past. At least six ages, or cultures, have left their relics in Oklahoma, and six linguistic echoes remain. There were many Indian tribes throughout the long past and traces remain even into the recent past and the present. These tribes have intermarried with the settlers, as I have said, and they are no longer pure Indians, although they treasure their Indian legends. Oklahoma, although young as one of the United States, is old in her relations with white men. Francisco de Coronado of Spain, in search of gold, marched there in 1540. In the

1700s Oklahoma was part of the Louisiana Purchase, and in the next century was part of the territory of Missouri.

Today she is a prospering, beautiful state, with many industries, oil the most important. Her climate is so good for agriculture, however, that she can grow almost any crop. She is rich in parks and recreation spots, in schools and colleges, in writers and artists and in music, particularly of the folk and country variety. But most of all, her people are enjoyable. They love to tell tall tales and sing songs. They have produced important singers.

And for a last memory, my friend and neighbor in Bucks County, Pennsylvania, Oscar Hammerstein, wrote a musical famous around the world and, to this day, it carries the name of this lovely state everywhere——OKLAHOMA!

OREGON

For years I had longed to see the beautiful State of Oregon. Its climate, its scenery, its delicious fruits kept me in a constant mood of temptation which I had resisted, however, because I could think of no real reason, except pure personal pleasure, for

traveling so far from homes in Pennsylvania and Vermont. Then there came a time in my life when I felt an obligation, as an American by long ancestry and birth, yet as one who by chance had spent most of my life in Asia, to set forth and tell the sorrowful story of those Amerasian children, born displaced by the chance of our times because their mothers were Asian and their fathers United States servicemen. I went to every state, speaking in some three hundred and fifty cities, and among these states was, of course, Oregon.

I approached Oregon from San Francisco, motoring northward and following the coastline of the Pacific Ocean. Though I have traveled on many of the famous scenic routes of the world, even the lovely Amalfi Drive in Italy on my way to Capri, I consider that drive along the coast to Oregon the most beautiful of all. And Oregon itself—how richly it fulfilled my expectations! The romantic scenery of sea, forest and mountain; the mild climate which encourages gorgeous flowers, particularly the rose, my favorite of all; the delicious and various fruits, all these combined to make this a state of pure delight. True, I wondered sometimes if the people of Oregon were able to realize what they possess. But of this I will not speak. It takes centuries for a people to realize and sufficiently love the beauty of places such as Oregon.

Politically the state is young, though its history is full indeed. Lewis and Clark were sent by President Thomas Jefferson to explore the region and to see whether the Pacific Ocean could be reached by overland. Oregon was, of course, part of the Louisiana Purchase. I wonder if young Americans today are sufficiently grateful to Jefferson or even realize his foresightedness in buying in the name of the United States the vast territory called the Louisiana Purchase! Ours would have been a sorry little nation had he not insisted and persisted against all opposition in thus creating a fitting future home for a great nation.

At any rate, Oregon was the end of the trail for Lewis and Clark. There before them was the Pacific Ocean. But other claims followed. John Jacob Astor with his fortune built on the fur trade, the Canadian Hudson's Bay Company which wanted to keep Oregon for England, and Captain James Cook, the English captain who saw the beauty of the Pacific coast in 1778 and even Russia, all contended, but it was Lewis and Clark who held it firm for the United States. Still, it seemed far away for settlers and they did not come in numbers until the nineteenth century after the Oregon Trail had been established in 1843. They came, those early families, to seek good farmland and not as miners to find gold. The first shipment of wheat from their farms left Portland and went to Liverpool in 1883, a notable year.

Returning to John Jacob Astor, for whom the town of Astoria is named, his historic fur trade began in Oregon after a long voyage around Cape Horn. When his partners had reached Oregon, they chose a spot overlooking the mouth of the mighty Columbia River, ten miles from the Pacific. It was very near the place chosen by Lewis and Clark for wintering.

Oregon is rich in forests, and she has great rivers. Although she is still proudly agricultural, she is also rich in electric power and manufactures, and since she is rich, she has had the means to develop culturally. Good schools, universities and art centers are part of her peoples' lives.

The state has one national park that is a spectacle of natural beauty and planned magnificence, Crater Lake. She has one splendid national monument, the Oregon Caves; one national historic site, McLoughlin House at Oregon City; and one national memorial, Fort Clatsop. To this I must add an annual Shakespearean Festival, at Ashland, accompanied also by a series of modern plays.

The town of Bend came, I was told, from the

farewell of a departing settler who, loath to leave the lovely area, cried out as his boat rounded the bend in the river, "Farewell, Bend!" The town was then called Farewell Bend but the practical post office department shortened the name to Bend.

I must, of course, return to the famous Crater Lake National Park. Any guidebook on Oregon will give details, seemingly extravagant but true, of this extraordinary work of nature. The lake was once aptly called Lake Majesty. The waters, deep and blue, lie in the crater of a great extinct volcano formed six thousand, five hundred years ago. Centuries of rain and snow have made it the deepest lake in the United States, nearly two thousand feet. The landscape surrounding it is formidably beautiful, and state authorities have done everything to make the lovely place accessible and comfortable for visitors.

My interest in sea animals leads me to mention the little town of Florence, where there are sea lion caves, the homes of sea lions in their natural environment. Some of these animals grow as large as twelve feet long. They can be seen quite easily.

Hood River is a small town in a wonderful, fruit-bearing area, from which come some of our finest fruits and in remarkable variety. It is an added delight that the nearly always snow-covered Mount Hood, Oregon's highest mountain peak, is part of the town's scenery.

I have left until the last my own private, personal, deepest concern in Oregon. In the town of Eugene there is one of the finest schools in the world for retarded children. The school bears my name. I consider this the highest honor of my life.

PENNSYLVANIA

It is very difficult for me to be impersonal about this State which has been my home for half a lifetime. I chose it because it was and is the central spot among my various activities. My Pennsylvania house is well over a century old. It is built, like many old Pennsylvania houses, of golden brown fieldstone—that is, stone of brown shot through with shades of gold. Such houses were built by the English who were among the early settlers in the state, and by the Germans who followed them. My house is in the eastern half of the state, equidistant to the exact mile from mountain, sea and city, all places important in the carrying on of my life.

Pennsylvania has no seacoast of its own but it is an hour or two from the fine beaches of New Jersey. Philadelphia is a port city by right of the Delaware River which flows toward the sea. It is true, though a cliché, that Pennsylvania has everything and more than most small nations have. This "everything" begins with history. The city was founded by William Penn, an English Quaker, and from him came the state's name. The Quaker influence, militantly mild, still prevails in

the state. The next influence in strength comes from the strong presence of the Pennsylvania Dutch, so-called because the word Dutch is a corruption of the German word *Deutsch*, which of course means "German." These major sources have produced an industrious, stubborn population, sure of itself and its ways.

Historically, too, the state is important because it was the first capital of the United States. In Independence Hall in Philadelphia, that architectural gem which stands between Fifth and Sixth Streets on Chestnut Avenue, the Declaration of Independence was signed in 1776. Benjamin Franklin made Philadelphia his city. His stout figure in bronze stands on top of the magnificent Capitol Building. It was long a legend that no building in the city should stand higher than old Ben Franklin but, of late years, the highrise building epidemic has stolen in. Philadelphia is famous chiefly for its fine Colonial architecture, in which rows and rows of beautiful town houses have their part, for its historic shrines and for its development in all the cultural arts. It has a magnificent museum, second only to the Metropolitan Museum of New York, and a symphony orchestra second to none; it also has the finest hospitals and medical research centers, and some of the best colleges and universities in the country. In its own dignified and aristocratic way, Philadelphia claims its preeminent position in age, history and culture in the United States. It is not an easy environment for the newcomer or the *parvenu*.

Philadelphia in the east and Pittsburgh in the west—they are not rivals because they are too unlike, although Pittsburgh has its symphony orchestra, too—but Pittsburgh is predominant in industry. Steel and coal once kept its atmosphere a murky gray and poisoned the lungs of labor and management alike. Now, however, the air is clean and the skies are blue again. A tremendous and heroic antipollution campaign achieved this magical result. The contributions of the Mellon family have done much toward making Pittsburgh beautiful.

Pennsylvania is the Keystone State in industry as well as in the arts, and in the fine Pennsylvania Dutch crafts and agriculture. There is no more refreshing sight in our country than the wonder-

fully tended farms of Lancaster County. Pennsylvania's forested mountains and splendid parks, the wide Delaware River and all the lesser waters, the wild areas contrasting with the sophisticated city life, her excellent educational system, all this means the state is a satisfying place in which to live, earn a livelihood and rear a family. So I have found it.

RHODE ISLAND

Rhode Island is our smallest State and the last of the original thirteen to enter the Union. As of a year ago, its population was just under a million. It has been said that it is a shy, withdrawn, modest

little state. True, its state flower is the violet, yet, in one era, it was the seat of an American aristocracy of fashion, wealth and pride, concentrated in the summer resort of Newport. The beautiful beaches continue to be attractive assets although Newport itself has declined and faded, like some of the beauteous and the proud who had made it their center. Handsome houses remain like shells of creatures once alive and flourishing.

Rhode Island, Rhode Island Red—the two names coincide in my memory of the twenty years I spent as the owner of a prosperous farm for prize Guernsey cattle; and as a side crop we raised the famous Rhode Island Red chickens, large brown fowl who produced large brown eggs. This breed was developed by the state's farmers at Little Compton, but I cannot find out anything else about that place.

Rhode Island itself is proud of its history and tradition. An Italian navigator from Florence, Giovanni da Verrazano, who was employed by France, had arrived at Narragansett Bay as early as 1524. Roger Williams fled to Rhode Island, driven by Puritan tyranny from Massachusetts in 1636, and two years later Anne Hutchinson and others followed.

Before Newport reached its prosperous heights, it had been famous as the town in which Roger Williams and his followers had taken refuge. Quakers settled there too, in 1657, an orderly, peace-loving people. The following year, a number of Jewish families from Holland joined the settlement. They built, in 1763, a synagogue famed for the beauty of its architecture. It is the oldest synagogue in the United States and is now a National Historic Site.

Perhaps the outstanding bit of Rhode Island's history is that she declared her independence of England two months before the traditional date of July 4, 1776. Rhode Island's independence day is May 4, 1776.

Ships, sailing, fishing and all things concerned

with the sea occupy Rhode Island. There are also some manufactures: toys, plastics, textiles. But the state's attraction is in the charm of its beaches, its boating and fishing. In present times Block Island is its chief resort. Its climate is delightful, summer and winter. It is a fair-sized island of twelve square miles, and it was named after Adriaen Block, who landed here in 1614. The history of the island has its macabre aspects—smuggling and shipwrecks—but today it is a prosperous resort, and farming and fishing, once its chief concerns, have taken second place.

Newport, I am told, is being divided into three parts: a United States Navy Base and Naval War College, a seaport and commercial center and a still fashionable summer resort. Wealth is not as resplendent in the resort area as it once was, but several wars may have left us all a more sober people, at least less flamboyant in our spending. For myself, I am interested in old buildings, and there are more than a few in Newport. For instance there is Old Stone Mill, once thought to have been built by early Norsemen, although this has since been disproved; Redwood Library, reputed to be the oldest library in continuous use in the United States; and Belcourt Castle, not old, but a great center for antiques from all parts of the world. The castle has sixty rooms and was once the home of Aline Hazard Perry Belmont.

The capital of Rhode Island, Providence, was founded by Roger Williams, who so named it in thankfulness to God. At first the center of a farming community, today it is a modestly handsome city of manufacturing and government buildings, libraries and museums, a very pleasant city.

There is something charming and delightful about Rhode Island. Its small size gives it the winsome traits of an exquisite miniature. Its people are kindly, stable and pleasant. There is less effort at competition. Instead, there is a mature enjoyment of life within known and acceptable boundaries.

SOUTH CAROLINA

My first journey into the State of South Carolina was to Charleston, and my memory of the city on that visit was of old culture in charming, civilized people speaking the English language with a slow, soft slurring of its consonants. This of course is the effect of long acquaintance with and influence by people of African descent. These charming white citizens of the lovely Southern city lived in beautiful white-pillared houses set in exquisitely cared for gardens that were fenced in, and with locked gates. Privacy and seclusion made the atmosphere.

There were, naturally, the magnificent gardens surrounding old plantation houses. The season was spring on that first visit, and not since I had been in the mountains of Kiangsi Province in the China of my childhood, had I seen such azaleas. The magnolias, those stately trees, I had not seen in such glory before. Somehow these trees, their glossy, dark green leaves set with great cream-white blossoms, symbolize the very spirit of South Carolina—beautiful, lush, pervaded with a scent so opulent that it borders in certain places on rottenness. There are swamps somewhere?

But South Carolina has magnificent beaches, swept clean by rolling surf. For some forty-two miles, Myrtle Beach provides an endless playground for many people. The sea is gentle, as everything seems to be gentle in this state, and there is almost no undertow. The very air is balmy for the Gulf Stream current sweeps close to shore here and keeps the winters mild and the summers almost cool.

I have made other visits to South Carolina and on one of them I spent days in travel to and fro by car, studying the landscape and faces of people. The landscape was benign, the people unhurried and perhaps without great ambition. Yet how do

I know what was in their hearts? I only know they moved with a sort of languor, they laughed easily and there was always time to talk. I concentrated that visit on Columbia, the capital, for I had gone there to trace the family story of a friend, intending some day to write it, although I have yet not done so.

The story began in a handsome part of the handsome city. The family was prosperous and in some ways even powerful. Their ancestry was distinguished. Then disaster fell, the fine house and gardens were sold and the family moved into a section of the city where houses were comfortable but not elegant and the gardens were smaller. In time, as decline continued, this house too was sold and the move was made to a still smaller house in a more crowded part of the city until, finally, the last home was a small apartment above a grocery store. Here a brave woman and her ambitious, talented son took care of a dying man. No, it was not the end of the story. That was in a burial ground, tangled with the weeds of a half-ruined country church. Two graves had no headstone. I stood looking at them, beside me the boy now grown to a successful, brilliant young man. We went straight from that churchyard to a nearby house where the verger of the church lived, and the young man ordered the finest tombstone to be had.

The story of three human beings had been unfolded before me on the visit and has stayed with me ever since. In a way it has typified for me the history of South Carolina, its early days spent in the rich glory of plantation life, its graceful pre-Civil War period based upon slaves, its postwar decline and then the rise of the fresh young life of a new day.

What that new day will be I do not know and perhaps South Carolina herself does not know. One fact impresses me very much, and it is that South Carolina is different from North Carolina to an extraordinary degree. This difference ex-

tends to the very air one breathes. South Carolina has the languor of Georgia and the far South. Rich and poor alike, and there are extremes in both, speak and move and live with a sort of mild, philosophical lethargy not to be found in North Carolina. How far does this languor eat into the mind and soul? I wonder!

SOUTH DAKOTA

My memories of this beautiful State date very far
back. Somewhere there in a hillside cemetery, a
little grave marks the resting place of a small
niece. She had been born in China, far up the
Yangtze River, but in her early years accompanied
her parents and brothers to the Untied States, the
family driven homeward by communist revolution. Her father's work took them from an eastern
state westward to South Dakota, where she died. I
have never been able to find her grave. Again my
reminiscences take me to the long camping trip
that our own family once took when our children
were in their early teens. I had read of the many
sights to be seen in South Dakota, including the

strangely beautiful Badlands through which we were traveling on a hot August afternoon. Then the air conditioning failed in our big chauffeur-driven limousine, bought new for the cross-country trip, and we sweltered while little Fords skipped merrily past us.

It was on that trip that we first saw the magnificent heads of the four presidents sculptured on Mount Rushmore. I saw them again only recently when we were driving an Amerasian student, half-Korean and half-American, to his western college. We stopped at Mount Rushmore at his request. It seemed that years before, when he was a small lonely orphan in a miserably poor Korean orphanage, he had somehow found an empty envelope, thrown away perhaps by an American soldier. On it was a United States stamp depicting the stone sculptured heads of the presidents. He kept the stamp as his greatest treasure, dreaming that one day he might see the reality. By chance of fate he was found and brought to the land of his father and so, finally, to South Dakota and to Mount Rushmore. I shall never forget the moment when he saw the noble heads carved out of the mountain rock. Tears shone in the Asian eyes in the American face.

"It is my dream come true!" he said.

But to memories I add what I have learned also in books. Of all our many states it may be that South Dakota is the most varied in landscape. Mountains and dust-ridden deserts, rivers and glacial lakes, a manifold agriculture, strange black soil that is unproductive and shifting in the winds, and pockets of rich farmland—the state seems to have something of everything.

The same variety appears in its population. It is one of our newer states, relatively, and its settlers were people from the East. It was a territory until 1889 and then was opened to homesteaders who were, for the most part, people of some education—teachers, lawyers, merchants and eager young men. They were accustomed to a cultural

background of education, music and the arts, so they created their own music and dancing and built their schools, churches and homes with a

modicum of decency and comfort. They found a number of Indian tribes in the region to whom they accommodated themselves, on the whole peacefully but not always so. Speaking of the arts, there is in South Dakota a woman, herself such a fine artist that I bought one of her paintings and

it still hangs on a wall of my Pennsylvania home. She lived alone in a cabin, not too uncomfortably, and she made doughnuts for a living so that she could continue to live and paint in South Dakota.

"Once you've seen its beauties," she said, "you can never leave."

The early American homesteaders were followed by an influx of European immigrants. They brought with them the ways of their origins and enriched the state with their inherited gifts. Norwegians, Swedes and Germans, they brought their own vigor to the new land and their old skills to enrich its life. They were welcomed by the earlier arrivals and the general atmosphere of the people today is one of easy friendliness to any newcomer. Together the people farm the land, carry on business, meet to hold discussions about books, to make music or enjoy a traveling theater group. They flock to concerts, bands and art exhibits.

My own, very first knowledge of South Dakota was in China when I read Ole Rolvaag's *Giants of the Earth*. Later, I read the sadly beautiful works of Hamlin Garland and still later, the novels of Rose Wilder Lane. But the state is rich as well in resources outside of books. Scientific excavations have revealed endless treasures of early animals now fossilized, and prospectors have roamed the rocky slopes of the Black Hills to find gold, silver and precious stones. The famous Homestake Mine has yielded more than three hundred million dollars in gold. Various ores are to be found, too numerous to be mentioned here, but enough to make the state a prosperous one. Several fine national forests contribute their share of riches in timber.

In short, each time I travel through beautiful South Dakota, I am impressed anew with the fact that it is a very young state, its wealth yet to be fully discovered and used.

TENNESSEE

My first knowledge of Tennessee goes back very far. I am eight years old, a little yellow-haired girl, living with my parents in China. Ours is a pleasant brick house, set on a hill overlooking the great Yangtze River. Usually the atmosphere of our house is quiet and orderly. My scholar father must live in peace. Suddenly, an interruption occurs. A gentleman from Nashville, Tennessee, is expected. It becomes necessary for me to find the State on the map of my geography book. Tennessee is in the United States. Nashville is in Tennessee. Why is this gentleman coming from so far? He represents the Presbyterian Board of Foreign Missions, under whose auspices we are in China. He is very important indeed. My intense curiosity makes me impatient. But when he ar-

rives, I am disappointed. He is a tall, lean man who is homesick for Tennessee. He does not like China, the Chinese or Chinese food. He is not even interested in Chinese Christians, it seems. He wishes only to go home. We are glad when he is gone.

I saw Tennessee for myself when I was at college in the United States, ten years later. I visited collegemates in their home in Memphis—charming girls, charming family, charming house. I understood why the gentleman had been homesick. All Tennesseeans are homesick, I am told, if they are not in Tennessee. It is a small state—relative, that is, to New York or Texas—four hundred and thirty-two miles east to west, and a hundred and twelve miles north to south. It is definitely a southern state, as one knows whenever a resident opens his mouth to speak. The state is divided into three parts: east, middle and west.

Forty percent of the people live in east Tennessee. It is rough country, made up of mountains and hills, and inhabited, I am told, by moonshiners and hillbillies. I do not know if this is true. I do know that tourists enjoy the scenic beauties of this area. It is a wild sort of beauty with an untamed and even untamable quality pervading. The mountain dwellers quarrel a good deal, draw their guns quickly and are prejudiced against blacks, strangers and revenue agents. Knoxville is the largest city but Chattanooga, a noisy town, is no small conglomerate. The area is developing, however. Third-grade schooling was the average educational level in the last generation but schools are changing the average.

Middle Tennessee is Bluegrass country. The farms are small but rich, and nicely kept. Their fruit crops are delightful; they produce fine cantaloupes and strawberries. Tobacco is also an important crop. The larger farms breed horses and cattle. I read that Nashville is the financial center here with a population of around a quarter of a million. There is still considerable feeling against the North left over from Civil War days, I am told, and it is directed particularly against rich men and Wall Street. Be this as it may, Nashville is the state's most modern city, its most sophisticated, and it contains the fine Vanderbilt University.

Western Tennessee looks north to Kentucky, west to Missouri and Arkansas and south to Mississippi. The land in the region is rich and it produces cotton and soybeans. Memphis is the center and Memphis I know from visits; my friends had been the daughters of a cotton king, from whom I learned all I know about cotton. Those were the days of Boss Ed Crump, a politician, feared, loved and hated, a giver of gifts when he chose and a dispenser of good or ill. I learned much about United States politics when I visited Memphis, and I was not surprised, but saddened, when later Martin Luther King, Jr. was murdered there. But there are many cities in the United States where this could have happened. Let me not delve into politics in any state.

Memphis is said to be the place where Hernando de Soto planted the Spanish flag on the banks of the Mississippi. Am I reminded of this because it was Jackson who named Memphis on the Mississippi after the Egyptian Memphis on the Nile? President Andrew Jackson, as we know, came from Tennessee—a good representative, if I am to believe history, of those hardy, hard-core days in his state.

I must, however, revive my memory of Senator Estes Kefauver, that good and simple-hearted Tennesseean, who helped me more than once when I needed it for a Chinese friend threatened with deportation. He was an honest man, this Senator Kefauver, at least towards me, and I do not qualify my estimate of him. He helped me to understand Tennessee as I might not have been able to do.

I recall, at this moment, that those magnificent and terrifying mountains, the Great Smokies,

are in east Tennessee. For those who love scenery that is truly scenic, here it is. There is also the great Tennessee Valley Authority project. I had visited it once when it was in the making and listened to the arguing pro and con. It seems to me at this distance of time that the pros have it—cheap irrigation, navigable waters, public power on a magnificent scale also cheap, and fine recreational areas. This inexpensive power, not incidentally, has changed Tennessee from a rural state into an industrial one.

"A place of individualistic, strong-minded people," one guidebook says of Tennessee. A state of contrasts, it goes on to tell me, a state of mountain ballads and city ballets, of mule-powered mills and atomic energy plants. In short, it appears to be a very American state, this Tennessee, and inhabited by very American people.

TEXAS

There are parts of this huge State which I have not seen. I am told that in east Texas in the spring, the ground is a carpet of color. The wild flowers are protected by law and each year there is the deep blue of the state flower, the bluebonnet, contrasted by the bright orange of the Indian paintbrush, amidst patches of violets and black-eyed Susans. Overhead, the branches of the dogwood and redbud trees blossom profusely so that one is surrounded by color. There is even a festival in honor of the dogwood at this time of the year.

There are still a few virgin pine forests where the trees grow tall and stately. I have been told that one of the large lumbering companies has

been engaged in the conservation and replanting of trees since the early 1930s, thereby protecting its own investment. I am also told that this same firm kept all its employees on the payroll during the depression even though the salaries were very small.

For the sportsman, the deer herds are large and healthy, and men come from great distances for the white-wing dove shooting in the autumn. The large water impoundments such as Lake Livingston, Lake Sam Rayburn and Toledo Bend have some of the finest large-mouth bass fishing in the country.

Texans are proud of their educational institutions. There are many small colleges as well as the large well-known universities and medical schools. Some of the universities place great emphasis on sports while others, such as Rice University, are more concerned with academics. And only recently has been the opening of the Lyndon B. Johnson Library at the University of Texas in Austin.

Houston is the largest city in Texas and has become mostly a business, space and trade center, although it also has an impressive section devoted to medical research and treatment. Houstonians are proud of their symphony orchestra and the Alley Theater flourishes from local support. Fort Worth prospered and grew as a cattle town and is still regarded as such while Dallas, its very close neighbor and rival, became a more sophisticated metropolis. Dallas boasts of having many fine museums, its own symphony orchestra and a theater-in-the-round as well as the very famous Neiman–Marcus Department Store. San Antonio, on the other hand, has retained its Old World charm, blending the customs and flavor of Spain and Mexico with those of the Wild West. History is strong in the old fort, the Alamo, where men fought for independence from Mexico. Victory was denied them but the territory did win its fight for independence in the end. And Texans are fiercely independent to this day.

The people who first settled Texas came from everywhere, but mostly from the countries of Europe and the eastern part of the United States. A large German settlement still exists in the area of New Braunfels where, each year, fifteen to twenty thousand people a day visit the *Wurstfest*, a German folk festival which has been held annually for one hundred and twenty-five years.

Texas is a large state and has such a variety of people that it is difficult to generalize about it. In fact, one cannot make a general statement about this state or its people.

UTAH

My travels have taken me often, and always by car, across the fabulous landscape of Utah. It is awesomely beautiful. I say to myself as I gaze about me, "It must take courage to live in such beauty." Here is not the comforting beauty of smaller, older states. It is the terrifying beauty of sun and moon and stars. Canyons—I see again Bryce Canyon, its pink spires and rounded domes rising from the great hollow between; the Flaming Gorge and its ever-changing colors; the startling shapes of the Gooseneck; the Natural Bridges National Monument—all this and much more has been often described and never well enough. Yet who can describe them as they really are? One can only return to the State again and again to see if they actually are as one remembers them to be—Lake Bonneville, for example, a prehistoric body of water that is still huge, although it is just a fraction of what was once a great inland sea.

It seems paradoxical that this strange, wildly beautiful landscape should be inhabited by a puritanical, disciplined group of people called Mormons. But there they are centered in Salt Lake City. It is a handsome town, set in a high altitude bowl encircled by mountains. When first I had visited it, the air was pure and clear. I breathed deeply. The last time I was there, years later, clouds of smog hung over the city. I cried out against such pollution and asked why it was tolerated. The answer was simple. Citizens had long besought industry to come in, and now that it had, they dared not protest. Alas, Alas!

I had the solemnly inspiring experience on that visit of speaking to an audience of twelve

thousand people. And after that, I was ushered
into the Mormon Tabernacle to hear a special con-
cert of the famous choir. The heavenly music
echoed through the magnificent building and for
an hour and more I was transported. How wise
was old Brigham Young! Driven from one place
to another, he said, "If there is a place on this earth
that nobody else wants, that's the place I am
hunting for." He saw the moonscape land about
the Great Salt Lake and he exclaimed "This is the
place!" The date was July 24, 1847.

The Mormons have been good planners.
Towns are well laid out. Streets are wide, and
there is space between houses for gardens and
lawn. Rows of graceful poplars provide wind-
breaks. Irrigation waters the dry lands, and of
latter years industry and forestry have been established and prosper. Mormons are astute businessmen, it seems.

Yes, the state of Utah is rich in strange and
spectacular sights. National parks show extraordinary rock formations and colors. Cedar Breaks
National Monument, for example, at an elevation
of more than ten thousand feet, has a vast natural
amphitheater four miles long and two and one-
half miles wide. I remember the surrounding
forests because they had bristlecone pines which

are the oldest trees on Earth, even older than the sequoias of California.

The town of Logan, the fourth largest city in the state, stays in my mind because of the fact that it was founded on the idea and practice of living entirely from what could be grown from the land. This aim continued until recent times when pervading industries came in. Nevertheless I thought, or imagined, that the children there looked healthier than elsewhere.

Brigham Young himself laid out the town of Ogden. It is a good example of the traditional Mormon style, wide streets, rectangularly laid and bordered by various sorts of trees, all very well kept. Generally speaking, I might here insert, the streets of the cities and towns of Utah are cleaner and less strewn with trash than the average American city or town.

There are too many handsome cities and towns in Utah to mention individually but somehow Provo emerges from my memory. I think because of its breathtaking setting. To the north is Mount Timpanogos, over twelve thousand feet high; to the south are the wild cliffs of the Wasatch Mountains; to the east is Provo Peak, more than eleven thousand feet high; and to the south is Utah Lake, set against a mountain background.

There are other spots as beautiful in Utah's spectacular way. Some day peoples of the world will hear of all these places of beauty, extraordinary and wild, and all the world will come to see America. On that day the state of Utah will take her place among those states to be visited and seen.

VERMONT

I sit at my desk in my Vermont home and, facing a window, I see a typical Vermont scene. A road winds up the mountain and beside the road in a narrow rocky gorge, there is a rushing brook. A group of school children walk down the road, swinging their strapped books. It is half past four in the afternoon. It is spring but patches of snow linger on the mountains.

Vermont is a country unto itself. Indeed for fourteen years after the declaration of independence, the State refused to join the Union and remained an independent republic. It is a small state, containing only nine thousand, five hundred and sixty-four square miles, and hence is forty-second in size among its fellow states. To compensate for its small size it is, I dare say, the most ruggedly individualistic of all of them, and the influx of visitors, now that it has become important in its recreational facilities, seems only to accentuate the ruggedness of the native Vermonter.

Perhaps the mountains have shaped the character of the people. Vermont has several mountain ranges, although it is commonly spoken of as the Green Mountain State. True, the Green Mountains contain the highest peaks: Mount Mansfield, Killington and Camel's Hump, but there are also the Taconic Mountains, an older range geologically; the Granite Hills, which contain one of Vermont's resources; and there remain the Red Sandrock Hills, these last in the Champlain Valley. From these many mountains flow the rivers, the Connecticut River being the largest and longest and, until recent years when dams controlled its overflow, the most rampant with floods. In its own New England fashion, Vermont is perhaps the most picturesquely beautiful among our eastern states.

The people who settled here in early times were for the most part English and, except for some Irish, there has never been any great influx of other peoples. The names of cities and towns are English as are the temperament and physical characteristics of most of the people. The landscape, too, is like England in its green and rounded contours; the climate is cold in the winter but not too bitterly so while the summers are of moderate temperatures. Flowers abound; they are not tropical in their beauty, but gentle in color and shape. Autumn is another matter. Then the forested hills, mountains and the wide valleys between blaze with such color that tourists flood the area to see the show.

Historically, there had never been great numbers of Indians in early Vermont. The area was used as hunting grounds by many tribes but not as battlefields. Samuel Champlain, a Frenchman exploring Canada, was the first white man to see Vermont territory, in 1609. The Indians, attacked then by the French, rose up and drove them away from the area. Lake Champlain, named of course after the discoverer, does not belong exclusively to Vermont, however. The state owns its waters in cooperation with the state of New York and the province of Quebec. Aside from geography, Vermont has had a noble history. She was always against slavery, sometimes so intolerantly so that a Georgia resolution, prepared in exasperation, suggested hiring enough Irishmen to dig a deep ditch around Vermont and letting the independent little state float off to sea! Of all the wars they were called upon to wage, Vermonters fought most willingly and heartily in the Civil War. It cost them dear, for five thousand, one hundred and twenty-eight men died and the state contributed more than nine million dollars to war funds—no small figure in those sparse days!

In resources, farming and quarrying were the most important and winter sports and summer tourism have begun to show substantial returns. Grain farming, milk and cheese-making, maple syrup and sugar, are the state's chief agricultural products. Marble, and to a lesser degree, granite and sandstone were and are the greatest treasures. Fine buildings throughout the nation are built of Vermont stone, including government buildings in Washington, D.C. Marble comes in several shades but white is probably the most commonly used.

In so picturesque a state it is inevitable that writers and artists should gather, and such has been and is the case. Vermonters have not neglected education and the arts, and although they could not afford great consolidated schools, they have been wise in keeping children in smaller groups, simpler buildings and closer to life and nature. There are distinguished small private schools and colleges, and the University of Vermont is well known in the educational world. Quality rather than size has been the Vermont tradition. Artists and writers have found in Vermont a congenial atmosphere in which to work.

All in all, Vermont is a jewel state, small but precious.

VIRGINIA

This beautiful State is so much a part of my family's personal history that I scarcely know how to separate the personal from the national. To Virginia my paternal ancestors came, for religious freedom, in pre-Revolutionary times. They were among a group of Germans who bought large tracts of land along the Shenandoah River in 1740, and they belonged to a Presbyterian congregation, the first or second in Virginia. One or two brothers among them fought under George Washington; the other was crippled from some early accident. A century later my maternal ancestors left Holland, alas, also for religious freedom, and settled in what was then Virginia. Both families were shocked when, at the time of the Civil War, a boundary line drawn near their

educated in Washington and Lee University in Lexington. This city was the home of General Robert E. Lee and General Stonewall Jackson. It is a lovely town set against a background of mountains. George Washington had established Washington and Lee by giving it two hundred shares of the James River Canal Company in 1798. The university took his name thereafter. General Lee was its president from 1865 to 1870 and, after his death and burial in Lexington, the university became known as Washington and Lee. My brother attended there, too.

My own college education was also in Virginia, at Randolph-Macon Women's College in Lynchburg. It is situated on a high bluff above the beautiful James River. While I have forgotten

estates divided them from Virginia and placed them in West Virginia. Their sympathies were with the South, and in defiance of the fact that West Virginia had announced itself on the side of the Union, four of my uncles fought on the Confederate side.

Years later my father and his six brothers were

much that I learned there, I have not forgotten that town built on hills so steep that the women were said to be hunchbacked from going uphill and knock-kneed from coming down! No, my memories are of the beautiful Blue Ridge Mountains, of weekend canoeing on the benign river, of visits to the university in Lexington at the invita-

tions of young men attending there. I may be forgiven for remembering long, lovely afternoons rather than mornings spent in classrooms. Nevertheless, I do remember that this was the first accredited college for women in the state, and that it has a fine collection of art there and a tradition for art.

Charlottesville, near where Jefferson built his beautiful home, Monticello, is the present hometown of many of my cousins. It is a lovely place, dominated by the University of Virginia which is enclosed behind a remarkable serpentine wall. The university is a rival to Washington and Lee, and was the life work of Thomas Jefferson. Edgar Allan Poe was a student there.

Aside from this, what is Virginia? Historically, it is our oldest English colony. It was first settled in 1607, at Jamestown. The atmosphere of English aristocracy prevailed in graceful ways of life and to some extent still prevails in fine old mansions and courtly manners. The first legislative assembly took place in Virginia in 1619 and the first armed rebellion against England in 1676. The fundamental documents of the new nation bear the influence of men of Virginia: the Declaration of Independence, by Thomas Jefferson; the Constitution of the United States, by James Madison; the Bill of Rights of Virginia, by George Mason, served as the model for the Bill of Rights in the Constitution of the United States. George Washington, a Virginian, led the Revolution and was our first President of course. Much later the capital of the Confederacy was in Virginia and much of the fighting of the Civil War was performed in this state. Rereading the history of Virginia recently, I was impressed by the benevolent attitude of the early settlers toward the Indians. In our present national mood of self-flagellation, we encourage ourselves to feel guilty toward the Indians in our country. The early settlers in Virginia treated the Indians with courtesy and even sympathy and undertook schools for their education.

The dignity of history and the grace of an aristocracy at first English and then American still linger in this state. Originally Virginia was much larger in geographical size than it is now. Indeed, it then included about one-tenth of the area of what is now the whole United States, a vast territory. Today it is thirty-sixth in size among the states. Yet it has a magnificent diversity, a seacoast so indented that there are many fine harbors and wide coastal lands which are rich and arable.

The Piedmont area, spreading to half the state with its rolling hills, is superb farmland. Tobacco is one of its chief crops, but fruit orchards and dairy farms abound. The area rises steadily to the beautiful Blue Ridge Mountains; beyond them is the famous Shenandoah Valley where the land is rich in productivity and, alas, also in sad history, for here some of the bloodiest battles of the Civil War were fought for four long years. I ought to say that industry prospers, too, in this diversely gifted state, for the Piedmont area has many industries such as shoes, paper products, furniture, transportation equipment, glass and clay articles. The largest single-unit textile plant is here, too, in Danville.

All of these facts are true, but for me Virginia is memorable because it is beautiful in landscape and in ways of life. There is an atmosphere of repose and maturity, a grace that comes only with age. The state is rich in fine roads and beautiful parks, in mountain scenery and lovely historic towns. The Skyline Drive, though sometimes terrifying to a person who suffers from fear of heights, is safe and accessible by five roads, and rivals Italy's Amalfi Drive in beauty. State and Federal governments have united to establish other beautiful parks, historic sites and restorations, notably the ones in Williamsburg and Yorktown. Virginia's parks and recreation areas are

not raw and strewn with trash. There are signs of commercialism, as for example in the magnificent Natural Bridge which, the last time I saw it, was lit in the evening with changing colored lights while music echoed in its rocks. A voice read meanwhile the story of the Creation, contained in the first chapter of Genesis. Commercial—yes,

but even this was done with taste and some dignity and perhaps had its good effect.

Maybe my memories of years spent in Virginia among gentle, courteous people create for me an atmosphere congenial to me because I grew up in the ancient atmosphere of China, where people were gentle and courteous too.

WASHINGTON

The State of Washington, for me at least, is the gateway to Asia. There in the great seaport of Seattle the jets take off for Tokyo, and the freighters and passenger ships steam out to Hawaii and Japan. North is Canada and in Canada is Vancouver, a port to and from which my family came and went to China. It is a mighty state, this Washington, larger than the whole of New England but with far fewer people per square mile. Stay—I have another recollection having nothing to do with memories of childhood. I knew the Hanford Engineering Works through my friendship with atomic scientists. Here at Hanford was manufactured from uranium the plutonium essential for making the atomic bomb which ended World War II. In the midst of the wild beauty this was done!

And now another memory creeps up from the past. A favorite picnic place of my childhood summers was near the giant gingko trees in the mountains of Kiangsi Province in far away China. The Big Trees we called them—huge, living trees in an ancient country that regarded them as sacred. But in Washington, a young state in a young country, I saw gingko trees so old they are petrified in stone. I read that this dead forest had been formed by the flow of lava over fallen gingko trees.

Life is abundant nowadays in Washington state, the life of a new country. Fish abound in the streams and in the mighty Columbia River. The blue-black trout are found only in Lake Crescent —I do not know why. But there are many species of fish found elsewhere. In the forests, big game had been plentiful until state bounties decimated the number. And among small animals, I note especially the shrew mole, which is neither shrew nor mole altogether but something of both; I am

told it is a creature of ancient Asian ancestry. And of birds, I read that the Chinese pheasant was introduced here in 1880, a bird beautiful to see and delicious to eat, as I remember again from childhood days when pheasant were always in the Chinese markets.

Other gifts to Washington were not only introduced from the Orient. The Douglas fir was the gift of David Douglas, who introduced it to Europe in 1827 and thereby established a vast commercial asset to the state. There are other conifers of various kinds which have been forested and reforested again and again to grow more crops, so that even today one may walk or ride for miles between green walls that meet above one's head.

Nevertheless, Washington is often reminiscent of other parts of the world, even of the tropics. I am especially interested in ferns, perhaps because of my childhood in subtropical countries; and I have seen rich fern life in this farthest state of our Northwest, an area which really has nothing to do with the tropics except for the warm ocean current that tempers its climate. The sword fern in Washington, for example, grows sometimes as high as four feet, and the tall brake and delicate maidenhair ferns are exactly the same as those found in the inland province of Kiangsi in China. Orchids, too, are plentiful. Indeed, the climate encourages many flowers and much rich foliage, but perhaps the most beautiful is the rhododendron, which is the state flower.

As is the case with so many regions in our country, fortunate people that we are, in addition to great forests, rich fisheries, fertile fruit orchards and farmland, Washington has varied mineral deposits and ample power resources. What of the people, however, who enjoy these benefits? The first people, of course, had been the Indians.

There was no unity among these Indians. They were as two major groups, separated by the mountains of the Cascade Range, and there were many tribes within each group. All Indians alike were being overwhelmed by the enterprising and aggressive settlers, but the Indians of this region were not as easy to overwhelm as they had been in other areas. Here was an organized society with an inherited nobility, upper and middle classes and a slave group lowest of all. Over these a chieftain ruled. It was a paternal society, with the line of descent through the father.

Nevertheless the white man prevailed. In the early part of the eighteenth century, Peter the Great of Russia determined to occupy all territory in North America not preempted by others, and his successor, Catherine the Great, sent a Dane, Captain Vitus Bering, on two explorations. The explorer discovered the strait named for him. Russia held Alaska, and Spain and England clashed for a time over the Northwest. Spain withdrew and the Oregon Territory, as it was called, then became a source of contention between England and the United States. Settlers moved into the great area, especially after the discovery of gold in the nineteenth century, but statehood for Washington was not established until 1889. By that time, the Indians had been pushed back or decimated by local wars and treaties.

Washington is a glorious state, rich in beauty and resources. Her people have developed industries, transportation and every modern convenience. Education is of the best, beginning with its first school in 1832 to the well-attended state universities of today. Private colleges remain on the small level, for the most part. On every front, however, Washington continues its spectacular modern growth.

WEST VIRGINIA

West Virginia has always been a personally important and interesting State in my life for it was there that I was born. My paternal and maternal ancestors had settled there in pre-Revolutionary times, and there the two families have remained ever since, except for those wanderers, my parents. In my own time, frequent visits to that beautiful and mountainous state have induced me to believe that West Virginia is only beginning to realize and move toward the fulfillment of its potential. The publicized appeal of poverty in the regions of Appalachia have misled us into thinking of West Virginia only as a poverty-stricken state. Its poverty is due to the lack of development of its extraordinary natural resources. These resources are not only valuable but extremely varied. Coal, natural gas, salt, electric power, oil, coin nickel, chlorine, glass, limestone and forestry are only a partial list.

The human resources are as varied. West Virginians are made up of every type of human being: the hillbilly, the miner, the industrial worker, the farmer, the merchant, the industrialist, the graduates of fine universities, the aristocratic families living in mansions with histories of great forefathers—all are to be found in West Virginia. They share one trait in common, however; they are fierce individualists.

Variety, variety—and this extends even to the climate. In general, it may be said to be humid, except in the mountains, but it ranges from cold winters and hot summers, to the ocean-touched calm of the Eastern Panhandle. Rainfall is ample, especially in the mountainous areas that are in the greater part of the state. Variety, too, is to be found in the animal and bird life. The birds of

Canada pause to nest and breed in the high Alleghenies, and birds from the South linger and live in the lowlands. Flowers are many and manifold, more than two hundred varieties, it has been estimated, and the variety in trees is almost as great. In the Cranberry Glades of Pocahontas County, the county where I was born in my great-grandfather's house, there is an unusual, indeed unique, terrain. It is a glacial bog, where rare trees, shrubs, lichens and fungi grow. There are also terrestrial orchids and a very rare carnivorous plant, the sundew. This area is the mecca of many tourists and is well worth seeing.

West Virginia is, of course, the most important producer of soft or bituminous coal in the nation. This brings human problems to miners,

who suffer from an occupational disease known as "black lung." It is too optimistic to think that this ailment will prevent coal production, however, although it is estimated that at the present rate of production there is enough coal to last for four centuries more. The manufacturing of chemicals and synthetics is being developed, and there is no reason why West Virginia should not be among the richest states in the Union.

My judgments of my native state must, of course, be colored by my personal experiences there. My forefathers on both sides were among the most fortunate. Politically my paternal ancestors, accustomed to Virginia and Virginian ways, sided with the Confederacy, and four of my uncles fought in the Confederate Army. They owned rich land around Lewisburg and were far from the mines and the poverty. They were educated at fine schools and universities, and today are among the so-called well-to-do. It is inevitable, since my maternal family was equally fortunate and in addition became musicians and artists, that my views and opinions regarding West Virginia are biased. I believe there is nothing to keep the state poor or backward. The people as I have known them are energetic, intelligent and of strong warm nature. I resent the notion that poverty and backwardness are endemic to West Virginia. To me it is a state ready for progress in every area—ready and able.

WISCONSIN

My first acquaintance with Wisconsin was by way of cheese. In this food I am somewhat of a connoisseur. I say this for I learned about cheese long ago during a famine in China. A shipload of cheese had arrived from cheese manufacturers—perhaps in Wisconsin? At any rate, it was to be used as food for the starving Chinese. Unfortunately the Chinese preferred to starve rather than eat the cheese, which was strange to them.

And they would not tolerate it when they heard it was made from cow's milk, which they considered inhuman to drink. The small American community in China, among them my parents, had then mustered enough funds to buy the cheese in exchange for equal value in rice, thus saving the Chinese lives. Our cellar was full of cheese for many years and I grew accustomed to its constant presence on our table. Wisconsin, then,

seemed familiar to me even upon my first visit to the State. It is of course the dairy center of our country, producing sixteen percent of our national dairy products, and its cheeses are very fine.

Wisconsin gets its name, as so many of our states do, from an Indian word, *Outsconsin,* which means "where the waters gather." It is a very suitable name for here the waters do gather in some nine thousand lakes and fifteen hundred rivers, all teeming with fish. With all this for sports and recreation, the state has also about five million acres of national forest. Short summers and long snowy winters have resulted in winter sports of first-rate quality.

Wisconsin produces, of course, much more than dairy products. It is famous for fine Milwaukee beer, for those who like beer—and many do. Strangely, I have seen rice paddies in this state that reminded me of the rice paddies surrounding the hill in China upon which our house was built. And in these Wisconsin rice fields our own American "Asians," the Indians, were paddling in canoes. What were they doing? Gathering wild rice! There are many Indians in Wisconsin and I discovered they have beautiful forested lands in Menominee County.

The northern part of Wisconsin is brilliant with contrasting colors, white snow and blue sky, extravagantly hued sunsets, sudden quick-blooming flowers, dark thick forests. There is in one place a curious stony area, natural, I am sure, which has been called "a disorderly Stonehenge," although it was named *Ymer's Eyebrow* by Norsemen. It is a rocky area and beyond it are many lakes.

The largest lake, however, is below Green Bay in the east. It is Lake Winnebago, and on its western shore is the important city of Oshkosh. Every western or even midwestern state has its mountains to give variety to the landscape, and Wisconsin is no exception. In the distant north is the Mesabi Range, famous not only for beauty but

especially, perhaps, for its brilliant show of northern lights.

To return to Oshkosh, this city took its name from an Indian chief. As a child I remember studying American geography and finding it difficult to believe a city could have this name. I forbear to repeat my childish remark to my mother —something about its sounding like a sneeze—to which my mother replied with dignity that Oshkosh was a very important city, that it was also known as the "sawdust" city because it had so many sawmills. Now, of course, I know that it is not only near beautiful Lake Winnebago, but it is a very important manufacturing center for many products. The excellent Wisconsin State University is there and the Paine Art Center and Arboretum.

The name Prairie Du Chien had intrigued me on one of my trips through Wisconsin. The place had served long ago as a French trading post, and the trappers and explorers had named it after an Indian chief's dog, Alieu. There is an amazing house in this town built by Wisconsin's first millionaire, Hercules Dousman, who was an agent of John Jacob Astor. It has been well restored and is one of the local sights. Two presidents were involved with the history of this town: Jefferson Davis, President of the Confederacy, and Zachary Taylor, President of the United States. Both were connected with forts here, Fort Shelby and Fort Crawford, used in the War of 1812. The forts are built on an Indian burial ground and they are very old and very big.

Richland Center I remember as the birthplace of the great architect, Frank Lloyd Wright. He designed in 1918 a warehouse for a firm here. It had its own cooling system and this was considered in those days a remarkable and modern invention. Later the architect built his home, *Taliesin,* and his school, *Taliesin Fellowship,* at Spring Green. This is a small town, scarcely more than a village, but he made it famous and here is buried.

I must add that there is another very outstanding house, *House on a Rock,* designed and built by Alexander Jordan. It stands on a rock hundreds of feet above a valley and within this house are waterfalls, trees and pools. I do not know what Frank Lloyd Wright thought of it. It is now a museum.

In sum, Wisconsin is a beautiful state, rewarding to visit. Like many other states, it is rich in resources, including forests which, once recklessly destroyed, are now being restored. But industries are prosperous, and there are also rich lead mines.

The people are of diverse origins, with a strong underlying strain of Swiss, Scandinavian and industrious Germans. Yet one finds French names too, left behind by the early French explorers. And Senator Robert M. La Follette, that progressive leader who did so much to improve the laws of our country, came from Wisconsin, one of the many great citizens this state has produced.

The air of Wisconsin, at least for me, seems pure and rare and free of desert sand and tropical swampy heat. Perhaps I have seen too much of barren country and lowlying tropics. I like the clean cold of northern country.

WYOMING

My first experience in and with Wyoming was a lecture engagement in Cheyenne. As usual, I had traveled thither by car, absorbing everything I saw and heard on the way. When I reached Wyoming, however, it seemed to me I had been there before. I knew I had not, and after reflection I decided the feeling of familiarity came from having seen now and then, though not very often, the television westerns. Wyoming is a good "western"—not trashy or contrived but quite beautiful. Thus having established its identity, I enjoyed it with a free mind. I enjoyed its mountain scenery, its wide prairies, its clean towns.

Someone, somewhere, at some stopping place on my way to Cheyenne, called it the Equality State. Upon inquiring, I learned that this name came from the fact that Wyoming

women are what the Asians would describe as "strong." I remembered then that in the westerns I had occasionally seen on television, the women were indeed depicted as "strong." Frail and beautiful, or tough and old, they bossed men around, even men with guns, and men were polite and said "yes, ma'am" to them. Investigating, I found this was true. Women in Wyoming are indeed "strong," and men are polite with them and let them have their way to an amazing degree.

Thus Wyoming was the first state to grant women suffrage. That was in 1869 when Wyoming had not yet even become a state. In 1924, Wyoming was the first state to have a female governor. Her name was Nellie Taylor Ross. But before that, Wyoming was the first state to have women jurors and a female justice of the peace. It is a *non sequitur,* but Wyoming, I was also told, has more cows than any other state. There are three times as many cattle as people, at any rate, and six times as many sheep, in case one is interested in such statistics.

To return to the brave Wyoming women, it is natural that these women, being in power, should advance to a high degree the cultural life of their state. Good schools, a fine library system, the excellent University of Wyoming and the preservation of historical landmarks—these are some of the significant achievements of Wyoming women—all honor to them.

When finally I had reached the capital city of Cheyenne, after much loitering on the way to see this and that, and everywhere to listen and ask questions, I found a clean, spacious and uncluttered city in an atmosphere of bright sunshine and fresh air. Its altitude is something over six thousand feet, which accounts for the clear air. Cheyenne is the largest city in Wyoming, but it still shows the influence of cattle-ranching and western ways of life. It is, however, the business center of the state. Coal mining, oil and timber are also important resources of the area. The people are alert, intelligent, frank and kindly.

I enjoyed Cheyenne and hope to return to it. It is pleasant to visit a spacious clean city after the crowded, trash-cluttered old cities I have seen in other parts of our country. People can be clean and so, therefore, can their cities. Please, Cheyenne, do not change!

Of course I was interested in Cody, named after Buffalo Bill who had founded it. This town frankly makes the most of its traditions, perhaps with an eye to its proximity to Yellowstone National Park and the many thousand visitors who go there every year. This is entirely permissible for it is simply carrying on the spirit of that great showman. The Historical Center, bearing his name, is one of the showplaces of the town. There are also western exhibits and a Buffalo Bill village. I myself was interested in the Whitney Museum of Western Art and after that in the Cody Mural, which portrays the story of the Mormon faith. And of course there is a Buffalo Bill Park. Equally needless to say, there are annual rodeos. Naturally I went to one and was amazed at this dangerous sport. It was in Cody, Wyoming that I finally learned how to pronounce "rodeo" properly.

There are many wonders in Wyoming. Plucked out of my memory, I think of Devils Tower National Monument—the first national monument in the United States, as a matter of fact. It was so declared by President Theodore Roosevelt. This immense and towering natural rock formation stands upthrust by some subterranean power on a wooded rise. It is eight hundred and sixty-five feet high, and a metallic element in its structure makes it glow in different colors under the light of sun or moon.

Fort Laramie is a national historical site. I had to read its history to discover why. The fort served to protect the gold rushers, but before that it protected the early fur traders. Originally, it had been privately built by a fur hunter, Jim Bridges, and his partners; later the Federal government bought it to protect the expanding West from protesting Indians, who saw their lands slipping away to white men.

The Grand Teton National Park and Yellowstone are of course among the world's wonders. We approached them through the town of Sheridan, a pleasant spot named for General Philip H. Sheridan. In that town at a comfortable ranch, I spent weeks of quiet intense work upon my book, *My Several Worlds,* while my teenage children roamed the famous parks with a guide.

Wyoming has ever since been one of my favorite spots upon our planet, Earth.

DISTRICT OF COLUMBIA

Washington, D.C. is the Capital of the United States of America and to me it is the most beautiful city in the world. I confess that each time I visit it, which is regularly twice a year, I am there as a patriotic sentimentalist. Tears do not come easily to my eyes but I cannot prevent them when I gaze at the Lincoln Memorial. Once, when I stepped into that marble building, I really did see a little black boy curled in Lincoln's marble arms. I had thought until then that that picture scene was a photographer's clever trick. But there it was before my eyes.

The august and handsome city is composed of such a conglomerate of magnificent buildings that I believe it is not to be matched elsewhere in the

world, and I have seen most of the world's great capitals. It was designed by a famous French architect, Pierre Charles L'Enfant, in 1790. It has been the nation's capital since 1800 and the site was chosen, appropriately, by George Washington. Today it is one of the most cosmopolitan cities in the world, with representatives from every country in the world. Appropriately, too, it was one of the first cities to be desegregated and its present mayor is a black man.

The District of Columbia in which Washington is situated is not a state. It has no governing body. It is administered by a commissioner and city council appointed by the President. Its business is the Federal government. There is almost no industry except that which is necessary for the life of its ever-increasing population of government employees, national and international, and the services necessary for the thousands of tourists who continually stream through its streets and public buildings. These are mostly Americans, of course, and they come to see Washington not as strangers but as proprietors. This is their city, the seat of their elected government, the symbol of democracy everywhere in the world. They are deeply proud of Washington. School children learn here at firsthand how their government works and with this knowledge go home again to cities, towns, villages and farms, enlightened and inspired.

Every state in the Union makes a contribution to Washington, and not only through taxes. I sit writing this morning in a Vermont village but not two miles from my house is a great marble quarry. Out of that quarry has come the white hard stone for stately buildings in Washington. From our marble, the tombstone for the grave of President John F. Kennedy was carved. Something of every state has been built into Washington.

The great buildings there need not be enumerated here. They can be found in any tourist guidebook. My own connection with the city for

315

many years was as a Trustee of Howard University, that most famous of all the land-grant colleges in this country. It seemed eminently fitting to me that it should be situated in our capital. Primarily for black American students, the university accepts applicants from many countries, and of all races.

Of special interest, at least to me, are the many beautiful embassy buildings, housing ambassadors and their staffs from most of the countries of the world. In one capacity or another, I have visited a number of those embassies, and met and talked with their officials. It is gratifying to perceive the effect of our beautiful and dignified capital upon those who come to represent nations of their own. We can well be proud of Washington, and the District of Columbia.

317

EPILOGUE

Eight times I have crossed the United States from East to West. Uncounted times I have traveled from North to South. I have visited each State with the exception of Alaska at least once, and some I have visited many times. My purposes in such visits have been varied. Sometimes it was curiosity, sometimes to visit members of my family, sometimes to deepen my knowledge to serve as the background for a book or a story, sometimes to deliver lectures. Most often, however, I have simply traveled for pleasure. Included is my insatiable curiosity to know better, and in depth, my country and my people. I have still lived more years in China than I have in the United States. I have still known more Chinese than I have Americans. Therefore I am still eager to learn more, to see more, to understand more of my country and my own people.

While this is true, it is also true that I have not put into the pages of this picture book much that I do know. This is a book for pleasure, a book of remembering, a book of impressions. Text and pictures share this purpose. I did not, for example, put down the long, heart-searching conversations I had everywhere I stopped. I did not seek these conversations. People came to me with their questions and problems. Everywhere, people came to me. Sometimes, indeed very often, their problems were personal and their questions dealt with what to do. Retarded children, unhappy marriages, joblessness, despair, all these I met over and over again.

There were many other conversations, too. These dealt with national and international questions and problems. Our people are thinking large thoughts. How, they asked many times, how can we eliminate war from our way of life? Or, how can we build better relationships between the races, the generations, the sexes?

There were literally thousands of questions from young and old, men and women, intellectuals and working people. I found that our people are thinking people. They are puzzled but not discouraged. They are troubled but not hopeless. They are more humble than they used to be, but no less proud of their nation. If there can be any advantage in this sad war in Southeast Asia, it has been to teach us a new humility. All our military technology, all our superior modern weaponry, have served us naught in that arena. This I heard over and over again. It was followed by a question as to why this was so, asked not in anger or disgust, but with a lively curiosity and wonder, a new humbleness that was neither humiliated nor humiliating. Rather, I felt, it was the beginning of a new maturity.

I wish, therefore, as I close these pages of geographical and personal comment, to testify to a new faith in and love for my people. Faith and love I have always had, but on fresh acquaintance these are re-invigorated and re-enforced. I repeat, Americans are thinking in deeper, larger terms than ever before. They do not want territory, nor do they want colonies. They have no wish to control or to dominate other peoples. They do wish to, and they will, improve and modernize our own national life style. They understand at last— and it has not been a long last, for we are a very young nation—that we are one of a community of nations living upon one small planet, Earth.

I come home encouraged and hopeful. I am a realist, nevertheless. I am well aware of our national and international problems. But there is no reason to be discouraged. Our people, our magnificent people, are beginning to think.

Yes, magnificent is the word and not only for our people. I come back from these journeys to our many states, awed and overwhelmed by the natural beauty of our country. The variety is bewildering. The highest mountains, the deepest canyons, the wildest rivers, the greatest lakes, the widest deserts, the richest farmlands, the beautiful seacoasts, the vast resources in mining, forests, industry—we have everything.

How can we be worthy of such beauty and such wealth? In all humility I ask the question of my government and my people. The answer must come from us all. I might have come home discouraged, even frightened. But I am neither discouraged nor frightened. It is the people who make me hope, who encourage me to believe— *our people who are beginning to think!*

KEY TO COLOR PHOTOGRAPHS